Blue Jackets

Robert Livingston

Executive Press Ltd
Edmonton AB T6A 0H7
Canada
343-554-1210

The views expressed in this work are solely those of the author and do not necessarily reflect
the views of the publisher, and the publisher hereby disclaims any responsibility for them.

Paperback ISBN: 979-8-9895083-6-5
Ebook ISBN: 979-8-9913174-8-1

OTHER BOOKS BY ROBERT LIVINGSTON

THE SAILOR AND THE TEACHER

TRAVELS WITH ERNIE

LEAPING INTO THE SKY

BLUE JACKETS

FLEET

HARLEM ON THE WESTERN FRONT

W.T. STEAD AND THE CONSPIRACY OF 1910
TO SAVE THE WORLD

IN THE WAKE OF THE EMPRESS OF CHINA

THE FORGOTTEN CHAPLAIN

AXIS SALLY

THE TARNISHED ROSE

AMERICAN STORIES 1940 - 1960

THE ANCHOR AND THE JOURNALIST

TASTE THE WIND

A DEAN'S LIFE

A FEW VERY SPECIAL WORDS

This story is entitled *Bluejackets*, which focuses on Black recruits in the U.S. Navy during World War II. It is a sequel to *Leaping into the Sky*, which covered the creation of the all-Black 555th Brigade to determine if Black men could serve as paratroopers. As before, fiction and history are merged to dramatize "what happened" in a way that will pique the reader's interest and encourage continued engagement.

In this story, a young man attending the University of Washington is prompted by his grandfather to investigate a virtually unknown experiment conducted during the war (1941-1945) to determine whether Black men in the U.S. Navy could handle duty on a warship in combat. In researching the topic, the student will learn about two ships: the U.S.S. *Mason* and the PC 1264. The Navy's secretive "experiment" was conducted against a backdrop of racial discrimination in the armed forces, especially in the Navy.

Researching the topic will take the collegiate investigator to New Jersey, Maryland, New York City, and the Great Lakes near Chicago. Along the way, he will experience some very scary raft rides among ghost ships in a watery graveyard of discarded vessels. During this journey, he will also meet a lovely junior at the university's Library, who holds a secret related to the PC 1264.

As with the story of the Black airborne troops, aspects of this tale set at sea will not be easy to digest. The "ugliness" of racism in America's military was very real. However, by confronting this history, it is possible to learn from the past and make peace with it. This is important as we all struggle to create a better America for all of our people.

With love and affection,

Gramps, 2018

Contents

CHAPTER 1

ABANDONED SHIPS

SEPTEMBER 2035 – ROSSVILLE, STATEN
ISLAND, NEW YORK STATE

It had taken some time to find an opening in the 8-foot-tall sheet-metal fence that circled the graveyard, conveniently and completely obscuring the old dump site littered with abandoned ships, all sunk partially in the murky, shallow waters—abandoned and rusting away, scrapped reminders of an earlier, happier time.

So far, so good...

No need to deal with the large, rusting locks on the heavy, but decaying gate fronting this open-air mausoleum. And there had been no security guard to alert others of the intrusion, nor any laser-beam alert system to deter trespassers.

That was good. I silently thanked the gods of amateur sleuths doing quasi-legal academic research on the sly.

I had found the decaying ships. My information, hastily researched over the past few months, was accurate. Sometimes you just get lucky.

A few minutes later, I cautiously pushed my Mark IV Assault Raft through the gap in the fence and into the swampy, polluted waters of the inlet. Just enough room... Stored in the raft were the necessities of my venture: two cameras to record my findings, night vision glasses, bottled water, energy bars, and, most importantly, the sketchy, creased map I had copied at the local maritime museum, which, if true, would guide me to the ship.

It was time. I carefully stepped into the Mark IV, then quietly dipped my oars and began to row silently into a watery world of ghost ships.

A less-than-silent "acknowledgement" escaped my lips, a sort of backhanded prayer: "Thank God Dick's Sporting Goods had everything I needed, especially the extra-thick-skinned raft."

Out there somewhere was a ship I had crossed the country to find. Out there... somewhere... Would my luck hold? A vintage World War II vessel. A tangible reminder of what had happened so long ago. Evidence...

It was 5 a.m., and it was cold. Not bone-chilling, but uncomfortable enough with the wet mist that hung heavily around me. It would be another 35 minutes before the sun would appear in the east, first low over the Atlantic, and then circumscribing the New York State sky before vaulting westerly toward the Pacific Coast, where it would appear three hours later. For a short time, I would navigate in the lingering darkness, slipping carefully among the deserted, uninhabited ruins of vessels that had once plied navigable waters.

Time for the night vision glasses... Now, everywhere I gazed, I saw weathered dilapidation, rusting metal, and rotting wood. Once-proud vessels deteriorating in the oozing mud... Improbable metallic sculptures, stained by the inevitable saltwater corrosion, emerged uncomfortably out of the muck—an eerie, watery skyline.

ABANDONED SHIPS

This graveyard of ships smelled of decay. The stench was overwhelming, initially triggering a gagging reflex before the body acclimated to the putrid odors. This was a place of death, where ships came to die—and where I had come to find one metallic corpse before it, corroded and decaying, slipped too deeply into the muck, forever to be forgotten.

THE GRAVEYARD

Still, I thought, if these ships could speak, what stories would they tell of the officers and men who crewed them—of the sights they saw—of the dangers they experienced? That's why I was here, I reminded myself. If I could find the ship... then, if I could listen keenly enough, perhaps I would come to know her story and, in some small way, extract her from this grave, lifting her into the bright sunlight again to see her once more slicing her way through the waves, her battle flags unfurled and flapping in the breeze—a naval warship reborn.

That's why I was here. The fates had decreed it. Or Gramps...

Seven months earlier, in Seattle, I was angry.

I hated the V.A.'s intensive care facility. I hated the array of sophisticated instruments, the lifelines of blood, oxygen, and intravenous fluids—all keeping Gramps alive, if semi-consciousness could be called alive. I knew my 97-year-old grandfather was dying. The last heart attack had been too much for him. I knew it was time for him to leave me. And that's why I hated the intensive care ward.

My father, Matt, Gramps' son, had left earlier, as had others, to have a bite to eat in the hospital cafeteria. I wasn't ready to leave. I remained alone with Gramps, hoping that, at least once more, he would open his eyes, enjoying again a moment, as was his way with me, of intriguing clarity mixed with some mysterious undercurrent, punctuated by a large question mark.

And then, much to my surprise, Gramps' eyes fluttered open. For a moment, he stared long and hard at me before speaking.

"Still here, Garvey?" he asked in a weak, quivering voice.

"Yep."

"Sorry I missed your graduation. My old ticker..."

"Gramps..."

"UW grad... so proud..."

I tried to speak. The words wouldn't come. The tears did.

"None of that, Garvey."

"Gramps."

Amazingly, Gramps began speaking in a clearer, stronger voice.

"Now, don't get sentimental on me. You graduated—B.A. in American History from the University of Washington... Completed your M.A. in a year. That's what counts. And you did right by the 555th Airborne. Your graduate thesis really elaborated on what you researched in high school, as did the book you wrote—Leaping into the Sky. One hell of a story..."

"Thanks to you, Gramps, and your clues."

"And good old Professor Richmond. He helped. Still kicking, is he?"

"Retired... mentoring a few doctoral students. And fishing..."

"Good man."

"Like you, Gramps."

"Your mother ever forgive me for hauling your butt all over the country?"

"We only got to Kansas. And yes, you're forgiven."

I knew Gramps wouldn't be around for the book publication. Not if the doctors were right and the printers kept to their schedule. He knew it too. It was all I could do to hold back still another stream of tears. Damn... Why was love so painful? No. Not just the love. The loss...

It was true. My concerned parents had let Gramps off the proverbial hook—but only after a few last shots across the bow. "No more off to

'God knows where' with our son," Mom had cried out. "Enough of your adventures."

No, it hadn't been all that easy for them. Gramps had really pushed their buttons, watching, as they did, their high school son on a quest to unearth the lost record of the 555th Airborne, an all-Black paratrooper outfit in World War II. Spurred by Gramps' unbridled enthusiasm and cleverly posted clues, I had the adventure of a lifetime sorting through the past and setting the record straight about the first Black paratroopers in the nation's military history. It sure beat going to five classes each day in school. Every day... By a long shot... Every high school student should have an experience of this sort. Much better than the newest video game or a hyped movie...

Quite unexpectedly, Gramps, now exhausted, settled back into his pillow, eyes closing. I thought I was losing him again. Then, suddenly, with surprising strength, he gripped my hand, and with his eyes wide open, asked, "Chosen a doctoral topic?"

The truth was, I had a plethora of possible topics. And while each one was of some interest to me, not one of them had fully enticed me. Not really jazzed me... Got under the skin... This I had shared with Gramps weeks earlier.

I guess my face gave me away. A half-smile crept over Gramps' face, then floated away, leaving only an old man on his deathbed. And that should have been the end of it. But...

Still holding onto me, Gramps said in a halting voice, "Finish the story."

"What?"

"Garvey, finish the story!"

I couldn't figure out what he was talking about. Finish what story? The 555th Airborne? Couldn't be that...

Gramps released my hand. A moment later, he placed a folded piece of paper in my hands. As he did so, a slight smile again crossed his face, and he once more gripped my hand, saying, "Come closer, Garvey."

"What's this?" I asked, looking at the folded paper.

"A last clue."

"Gramps…"

"Finish the story… Rossville… Arthur Kill… Remember…"

Gramps slipped back into unconsciousness. And that was it. Later that night, he passed. Three days later, he was cremated. He had always contended that it was "a waste of good farmland to burden the soil with 'goners.'"

It was a while before I found the courage to open the folded paper again. With barely legible handwriting, he had scribbled PC 1264.

Gramps had indeed left me with a final clue.

CHAPTER 2

THE GRAVEYARD

I paddled slowly. Very slowly... I was in the watery labyrinth of the graveyard. The sun was rising, casting rays of light, shining brightly on some ships, leaving others darkened and certainly uninviting in the shadows. It was spooky as hell. I felt like these ships were haunted. By whom and for what, I didn't know. That I didn't speculate on... Not at the moment, at least. Around me, there was an eerie sense of stillness among the sheltered, rotting vessels. The waters were calm, lapping up against the relics with almost no wave action. This only added to my feeling of dread.

Around me were the lifeless remains of decaying wooden ships, steamboats, ferries, tramp steamers, small passenger ships, and cargo ships—all embedded in the mud, listless. Everywhere I paddled, there was jagged metal, rusted and dangerous to a rubber raft, especially with some wrecks submerged, while others were only partially exposed. And again, the smell... wood rotting, polluted and stagnant waters, the stench of rusted metal, the droppings of seagulls, floating sewage... All creating a witch's brew of toxic waters in the inlet where I floated.

ABANDONED SHIPS

I tried to remain vigilant... focused... Still, memories flooded back...

Rossville... that's what Gramps had whispered.

I knew it had to be a town. But which town? And where? A check of the Apple Cloud Matrix revealed seventeen towns named Rossville in the country. But which one was important to Gramps?

Gramps had said, "Arthur Kill." Who was Arthur? And whom had he killed? Had someone been murdered in Rossville? And what could this have to do with his admonishment to "finish the story?"

It took me a few days to figure out what was going on.

I continued to paddle quietly, smoothly, rhythmically, dipping my oars into the water, then pulling back gently—always alert to an old hulk, scuttled by its last owner, abandoned to the elements. One of over 200 ships stuck in the muck of the shallow cove between the shorelines of New York and New Jersey. Crowded together, the forlorn ships leaned against each other in a sad embrace of scraping metal and stained wood, always in motion, undulating as the indistinct, ubiquitous lapping waves brushed against them.

And everywhere, history... Old ferry boats that once carried New Yorkers to work and play. A railroad-car barge with an elevated wheelhouse, assuming a position that reminded one of a home on stilts... A fast fireboat that had once been a first responder in New York Harbor. In the midst of all this was a New England passenger steamer, the Eleanor Gay. Built in 1928... Ended her days at Normandy... D-Day... A British transport on that fateful day. Once gallant ships... now lost... discarded...

DISCARDED

Beyond the Eleanor Gay, the Eldia, a 471-foot merchant ship, was anchored just outside the cove—a new arrival. Unless a buyer could be found, the ship would be used for salvage, consigned to a pile of scrap metal. A furious storm had shoved her aground at Navsot Beach on Cape Cod in 1984. Now, only the seagulls waved to her, fluttering here and there, providing a last feathery salute to the old merchant ship.

But where was the ship I was looking for? It had to be here. Gramps' clues had led me here. Where was the ship?

It took me a while to make the connection—Rossville and Arthur Kill. Rossville was a neighborhood of Staten Island, New York, located to the west of Prince's Bay, on the island's south shore.

Arthur Kill was a tidal strait separating Staten Island from mainland New Jersey. More than that, Arthur Kill was a major navigational channel linking the "Garden State" to New York Harbor and was sometimes referred to as the Staten Island Sound. Polluted and nearly devoid of fresh water fish, and unsafe for swimming, it was Gramps' connecting link to Rossville.

The channel was approximately 10 miles long. It divided New Jersey's industrial sites from the island's salt marshes. Thankfully, Arthur Kill was not a homicidal character murdering wayward tourists visiting the "Big Apple." Far from it...

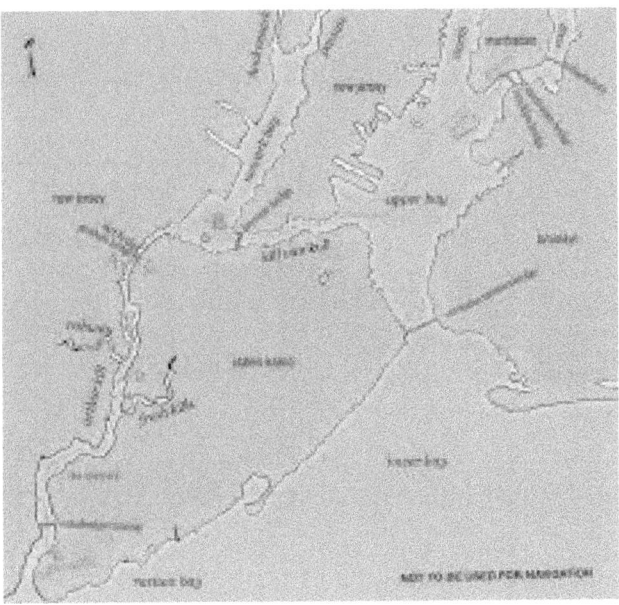

The name referred to the Dutch, who colonized the area before the British unceremoniously took it away from them in 1684. In Dutch, Arthur Kill was achter kill, which, when faithfully translated, meant "back channel"—a practical Dutch way of describing its location behind Staten Island. The English later Anglicized the words, transforming achter kill into Arthur Kill.

As for Rossville, it was named after Colonel William E. Ross in the 1830s. Among other things, Ross built a replica of Windsor Castle on a bluff overlooking the Blazing Star Ferry, which carried passengers from New Jersey to Staten Island across the Arthur Kill. Over time, the town evolved from an agricultural center into a hub of industrial activity and, more recently, a bedroom community for commuters.

The town and the channel were connected, but what were they connected to? Gramps, always one step ahead of me, had provided the clue: PC 1264. But what did it stand for? And the numbers—surely, they had a meaning.

The midday sun was high in the sky. Rafting on the Arthur Kill had become increasingly dreary, warm, and, as it seemed to me, fruitless. Though I continued to paddle, impatience and frustration gnawed at my hopes as the object of my search remained hidden, eluding me at every turn. Though he could be devious, I couldn't believe that Gramps would give me a false clue—that wasn't his style.

Eventually, I figured it out. The letters and numbers—PC 1264—stood for the USS Patrol Craft 1264, a patrol-class submarine chaser constructed for a singular purpose: to hunt down and destroy German U-boats operating off America's eastern seaboard. That was her reason for existence.

PC 1264

After a little research, I uncovered the basics about this ship. Her keel was laid down at the Consolidated Ship Building Company in Morris Heights, New York, on October 7, 1943. She was launched on November

28th of that year and commissioned into the United States Navy on April 25, 1944. She served with distinction until her decommissioning on February 7, 1946, at which point the Navy sold her for "scrapping."

But that never happened.

As fate and the twists of history would have it, she was stored in a marine yard near Rossville, Staten Island, adjacent to the Arthur Kill. Why this occurred, I was still piecing together. And yet, somehow, she had found her way here.

Somewhere in the flotilla of ruined ships lay the Navy's sub-chaser—larger than a PT boat, smaller than a destroyer. Somewhere in the crowded cove hid a vessel 173 feet long and 23 feet wide at the beam, still bearing twin depth charge tracks and a canopy bristling with 20, 40, and 50 mm guns. Somewhere in the tangled graveyard of lost ships was the USS PC 1264—still eluding detection, still guarding her secrets, and still defying the passage of time to cling to her anonymity.

THE ELUSIVE SHIP

———————————

I rested. I had to. I drank some water to slake my thirst and chewed on a power bar to quiet the grumbling in my stomach. I closed my eyes, telling myself I just needed a few minutes—a short rest. Above me, the sun boiled. I wondered how long I could keep this up.

My thoughts drifted.

"Gramps, I can't locate her."
"Keep looking, Garvey."
"You gave me a false clue."
"You don't believe that."
"She's not here."
"You're close. So close… Keep a steady eye."
"I'm searching for a ghost ship, my own Flying Dutchman."
"You're looking for the PC 1264."
"A phantom ship."
"The key to finishing the story."

There it was again—"finish the story." What story? The question jabbed at me, whirling through my mind as it had since that day in the V.A. It mocked me, heedless of my sore arms and cramped legs, demanding an answer I could no longer avoid.

I needed to remind myself the ship was real. From my shirt pocket, I pulled a picture of the sub-chaser, taken shortly after her commissioning. I scanned the image: the PC 1264 floated proud and trim, deadly in her purpose. Newly minted and painted, her name was etched on the starboard bow. Untested by battle and unscarred by enemy fire, she stood motionless at her berth, captured forever in the flick of a camera's lens.

She was one of hundreds of relatively inexpensive anti-submarine warships built to safeguard America's merchant fleets, larger warships, and troop carriers. Thin-skinned and heavily armed, she was a hunter, built to destroy the underwater menace of enemy submarines. Yet she had another role, less discussed but universally understood. Like a Secret Service agent sworn to take a bullet for the President, the PC 1264 was expected to take a torpedo to protect an aircraft carrier or a troopship.

None doubted that sacrifice, if necessary, would be made.

So common were ships of her class that no name was given to her, only a number. This was unlike other ships. Battleships were named after American states—like the USS California or the historic USS Arizona. Cruisers bore the names of cities, such as the USS San Francisco or the USS Juneau. Destroyers often honored individuals, like the USS Saufley, named for a naval pilot. Submarines carried the names of sea creatures: the USS Stingray, the USS Cuttlefish.

But the PC 1264 had no heroic name on her bow, no ceremonial champagne bottle cracked to commemorate her launch. She was simply a number, just another weapon in Uncle Sam's arsenal.

Yet Gramps wanted me to find her. To uncover her untold story. To finish a story.

But what story?

I drifted into a mist, cool and refreshing yet obscuring visibility. The current carried the raft while I rested, oars pulled from the water. The moment calmed me. Perhaps, I thought, the waters understood my quest.

Then—

I sensed it before I saw it. Something was out there. Like an ancient mariner, I gave in to the voice of the sea.

"Gramps, I think…"
"At last, Garvey…"
"Something's out there…"

Slowly, the silhouette of a large ship took form about a football field away. Not the lines of a merchant ship. Not the outline of a cruise ship. Something different. A dark shape. A conning tower. Guns.

It had to be the PC 1264.

I paddled now, faster than caution would advise, maneuvering around the hulks of other ships. At last, I came alongside her. Years of corrosive saltwater had nearly erased her name. Nearly. Rust had eaten away at her hull, tarnishing her once-sleek lines, leaving her a corroded hulk moored in an endless anchorage of despair.

And yet, in my mind's eye, she was still there: brave, defiant, plowing through the waves. Manned and battle-ready. An active ship of the U.S. Navy, still on duty.

I had found her.

The PC 1264 would live again in what I would write—honored, remembered, a brave ship with a brave crew.

"Gramps, I found her."
"Knew you could do it."
"Now what?"
"Finish the story."
"What story?"
"Always the same question, Garvey."
"And never an answer."
"The 'nigger ships,' Garvey."
"I don't…"
"Both ships…"
"Here? Another ship?"

"No. Scrapped in '47…"

"Where?"

"Finish the story."

Had I actually heard Gramps? Another ship… What other ship? Was he still pulling the strings? Silly question. Of course, he was. It was in his DNA to guide, nudge, and push me toward truths I hadn't yet grasped. With Gramps, I could never predict what was next.

Still, whatever my misgivings, I knew with absolute certainty I had to find the other ship. If I were to fulfill what Gramps had asked of me—finish the story—I needed to uncover this second mystery.

But first…

I turned my attention to the PC 1264. As I drifted quietly through the water, my paddles barely stirring the current, I surveyed the ship. I filmed her, photographed her, and jotted quick notes—thoughts and observations, perhaps for a future documentary.

Two hours passed.

I did everything but board the ship. I told myself that would come another day, likely with a team and the right equipment. That's what I told myself.

But the truth was something else.

I wasn't ready to disturb her ghosts. Not yet. But someday… Someday, when I knew more.

For now, I had what I needed. She existed. I knew where she was.

FOUND – THE PC 1264

(DIRECTLY ABOVE)

It was time to go home.

CHAPTER 3

HOME

A week later, I was back in Seattle, sitting down with my folks. I shared my research with them, showing pictures of the "graveyard" and the ship.

My parents, now approaching retirement, were in the education business. Dad worked as a school superintendent, and Mom ran a non-profit counseling service for at-risk kids. At the moment, they were giving me an unusual amount of rapt attention.

THE MISSING SHIP

"That's one heck of a story, Garvey," Dad said.

"That's what happened," I replied.

"You took quite a chance rafting around those wrecks."

"Calculated risk."

"But one misstep…"

"Hard to do that in a swamp."

"Good to see you've kept your sense of humor."

"Picked that up from Gramps."

"Gramps, still pilfering our son?" Mom chimed in.

"Mom…"

"Don't say it. That old man is still directing traffic around here, even from the next world."

"What are you getting at?" Dad asked.

"Now he's got Garvey looking for two ships—one in a murky harbor full of wrecks, the other somewhere over the horizon."

"There's a story here, Garvey?"

Dad caught on. There was a story. I wasn't going to debate the topic anymore. A decision had been made. I would follow my instincts—the PC 1264 and the other ship. I would, if possible, "finish the story."

"You didn't board the ship, Garvey?" Dad asked.

"Too dangerous to go solo. Just worked my way around her. Not easy… Lots of junk metal in the water. Always scared my raft would get ripped. Not exactly the place for a mid-day swim. Definitely not for a novice."

"But you know where it is?"

"Longitude and latitude to the last degree."

"You'll go back?"

"In time, yes."

"And you have some idea why Gramps wanted you to find her?"

"A glimmer—oh yes. And maybe a lot more."

"Care to share?"

Before I could respond, Mom cut in. "What about your doctorate? You need to focus on that."

"Mom, I think the old ship is my thesis. And maybe the other ship, too."

"How can you be so sure?"

I gathered the pictures I'd shown them earlier. After sorting through the pile, I pulled one photo out.

"Mom, the two ships are the key to finishing the story."

"What story?"

"Something linked to the 555th."

"The Black paratroopers you wrote about?" Dad asked.

"Right."

"How…"

"Look at this last picture, Mom."

"From the graveyard?"

"From the maritime museum in Rossville."

"Just sailors on the deck."

"Yes, Mom. But what ship?"

"The PC 1264. I can plainly see the numbers."

"What else? Look again. Look closely."

"At what?"

"The crew."

"Just sailors…"

"Mom… Dad… The sailors… They're all Black!"

CHAPTER 4

CONSPIRACY

SEATTLE, WASHINGTON, LATER

"I agree with your parents. You took quite a chance rafting in that maritime cesspool, Garvey."

"Had to be done, Professor Richmond. That's where Gramps' clues led me. Rossville and the Arthur Kill…"

"You could have avoided it. No one forced you."

"Gramps was insistent and dying. Did I really have a choice?"

"Pressure? Guilt?"

"Something in the middle. A self-imposed obligation to an old man."

"Whom you loved."

"He was Gramps."

THE CESSPOOL

The good professor nodded. We had grown close over the past few years, beginning with my high school research into Japanese balloon bombs and the all-Black 555th parachute experiment. As an expert on Blacks in the armed forces during World War II, he had helped me immensely in understanding racism in America, particularly in the 1940s. He had also encouraged me to enter the University of Washington, focusing on history as my major. Our relationship was something more than student/teacher but something less than father/son. Whatever it was, it endured and was satisfying to both of us.

I was in Professor Josiah Richmond's office at U.W., where stacks of books were seemingly everywhere—some neatly packed in cartons, others strewn about on the floor, perhaps awaiting the grabbling hooks that would end their days. A few ponderous volumes still clung to unruly-looking shelves, as if to say, "Just because you're retiring, why do we have to go?"

"Moving?"

"Retiring is okay. Packing is the unwelcome chore."

"You seem to have things under tight control."

"Garvey, your sense of the ironic and satirical is more than evident today."

It was my turn to nod. Looking around the room, I saw that the professor's files were bulging out of overly cramped cabinets, in addition to a myriad of unread student papers still cluttering his desk. His wastebaskets were littered with fast-food wrappers, the favorite being In-N-Out Burgers, closely followed by Chipotle's Mexican Grill. As with the ungraded papers, the culinary wrappers seemed to have multiplied. One might conclude that my mentor and friend was living in his office rather than merely working there in his last days at U.W.

For one anxious moment, an absurd thought passed through my mind, unnerving me more than I would have expected. The room reminded me of the Arthur Kill—only this time, books, not ships, littered the horizon, tossed and strewn about by the vagaries of U.W. bureaucratic rules governing retirement. The thought lingered and disturbed before I discarded it with a more pleasant, if not amusing, image.

Though the room looked like something out of Oklahoma's "tornado alley," it was good to know that my former professor still had class when it came to food on the run. Still, I wondered what had happened to his more organized scholastic bunker, which I had come to know quite well when pursuing my M.A. under his tutelage.

"The room, Professor…"

"You noticed."

"I'm a keen observer. Went to the Robert B. Parker 'school-of-go-with-your-gut instincts' every time, and keep your eyes open."

"Your father hooked you on Parker?"

"Gramps."

"I should have known. A real Parker fan, your grandfather, as I am to tell the truth. We spent a few hours now and then discussing Parker's plots and characters."

"You're a Spencer fan?"

"I leaned more toward Hawk."

"Figures," I said with a slight grin.

"It's a Black thing. As to your choice?"

"Susan."

"A wise decision. Smart, beautiful, gutty… Yes, a wise choice. Now, as to my room…"

Professor Richmond took a deep breath, glanced around the room despairingly, and wiped his brow before continuing.

"My decadence… My fall from the gods… This room… My apologies. Neatness has become controlled chaos. As to why… Well, two things. Obviously, leaving the campus after laboring here for twenty-five years… What can I say? You collect a lot of stuff… A lot of memories. As to the other point… I've also been desperately laboring to finish a book about Blacks in World War II. That is, in the military. And more to the point, Blacks in our Navy… Tried to finish before being ushered out by a '65 and done regulation.' Didn't finish the book. U.W. is giving me a few more weeks to clean up or get out, depending on one's point of view. They do want me to publish under their auspices. Very generous of the Huskies, don't you think? My work, their academic reputation… Unfortunately, there's no completed manuscript. As you can see, I'm having great difficulty with my exodus, if not my research. And the papers there from my last seminar… Sort of funny… Ungraded. And the students have already graduated. Higher education at its best."

I tried not to laugh. It wasn't easy. Professor Richmond, a giant of a Black man, showed no restraint, bellowing at his own sarcasm before getting serious.

"To tell the truth, Garvey, I need help."

"You need a snow plow in here."

"True, but I'll disregard that comment. What I need is a strong research arm. Someone who is interested in the U.S. Navy."

"John Paul Jones stuff, Professor Richmond?"

"Exactly. But how did you know?"

I smiled. At least my besieged mentor hadn't lost his sense of humor. As for my comment… My intuition was hard at work, or, stated somewhat differently, my Parker-gut feelings were telling me Gramps was hovering in this room. Of course, I didn't mention that. Not yet, anyway.

"To misquote our first naval hero, Garvey, 'I have not yet begun to finish my book.'"

"History will forgive you, Sir, as will John Paul Jones."

"You think so?"

JOHN PAUL JONES

I nodded again and said, "You're considered the expert on the topic. Blacks in WWII... You don't need a researcher."

"If only it were so. I have an Achilles' heel, and I'm afraid an arrow has pierced it—what we might call a dearth of research in a certain area of my labors. I guess I should have plunged completely into the River Styx. Might have improved my disposition and eating habits. I spoke to your grandfather about all this before his fatal heart attack."

"Gramps..."

"He was a self-made academic, you know. Knew a lot about the Navy, which is why I was speaking to him."

"Blacks in the U.S. Navy?"

"Precisely. But why did you say that?"

I, of course, suspected a conspiracy. What else could I deduce from the professor's surprising invitation to speak with him, and now this admission? They had talked. More to the point, they had conspired. I was now convinced they had plotted... Figuring out how to rope me into their devious plans. But truth be told, I wasn't unhappy they had talked, especially when I was the key to their conversation. With this in mind, I decided to leap headlong into the fray.

"Professor," I said with a shy smile and a wink, "I believe the two of you have joined forces to put me on the trail of the PC 1246."

"You're suggesting a conspiracy? Heaven forbid. Consulted? That, I think, comes closer."

"You teamed up?"

"Fairly stated, and for three good reasons."

I waited. Something was about to be said that would stir me to the core. Still, I could not anticipate what Professor Richmond said next.

"It's true we struck an alliance of mutual need. I needed help, as did your grandfather. You needed a doctoral topic, which we would provide. And lastly, your Gramps needed you to complete the story and honor a promise made long ago."

There it was… Gramps and his promises. What was it this time? Another pledge to visit the families of fallen warriors? Another book? Setting something straight? My grandfather seemed a glutton for self-inflicted punishment. Still, he was Gramps, and I loved him dearly. That old guy could get under your skin. I probably would have walked over hot stones if he asked.

The alliance bit I understood. Made sense. Two older guys navigating rough waters. And I did need a safe harbor. Make that a thesis topic. But the rest? It still made no sense. Again, complete what story? Fulfill what promise? Troubled waters… These questions I shared with Professor Richmond. His response was less than illuminating.

"Follow the clues, Garvey, and they will complete the story. That's what your grandfather hoped. As for the promise, I'm not at liberty to answer that question. Blood oath with Gramps… But the answer will come in time, I assure you."

Such clarity left large questions hanging. I realized the lack of information was the lure to keep me on the hook. Truth be told, I wanted to know the answers. Once again, my curious mind was waylaying me. Given that there was little I could do beyond nibbling at the bait, I changed the topic somewhat.

"Professor, as you know, I found the PC 1246. I also saw the photograph of the ship in the Rossville Museum. In an old display case lingering in the shadows… Hardly noticeable… Almost like it was placed there to keep it out of the limelight. Or, if I may be so bold, Professor, to keep it out of the history books."

"Your judgment?"

"Yes."

"Based on?"

"My understanding of racism in our military during WWII."

"Your work with the all-Black 555th Airborne?"

"And the crew picture I saw in the Rossville Museum."

"So?"

"An unusual crew... Men of color..."

"Officers and crew?"

"All."

I was beginning to catch on. Gramps, I'm sure, instigated by way of a text, lured the poor guy (my UW prof) with some tantalizing morsel about a lost ship. He bites. Responding, Professor Richmond visits Gramps. They talk. They plot. Next, Gramps whispers into my ear, conspiring to the very end in the VA Hospital. I bite. I head for the Arthur Kill, where I paddle my way into the past. And now it appears both Gramps and my professor wanted my help in "finishing a story"— "Blacks in the Navy." Had to be that.

These thoughts I kept to myself.

"Professor Richmond, you've been most kind to me, encouraging me to follow a history major. You labored with me to complete my M.A. on the 555th Airborne. You convinced me to be a T.A. while I worked on my doctorate. You even stifled my youthful rebellion against teaching in the public schools, or here at U.W. Told me it wasn't my fault, if I remember correctly, that my father was a school administrator and my mother was a counselor. And that my sister, Wells, was an elementary school instructor... 'Teaching,' you said, 'was in my bones. Stifle the insurrection.' Your words exactly... 'Give in to the inevitable.' And now this business with the Navy... What am I missing?"

"Keen as ever, aren't you, Garvey?"

I felt pretty good. Act dumb... Look confused... End with a question... And now it was time to push.

"What's really going on here, Professor?"

CHAPTER 5

CONFESSION

"The long and the short is this, Garvey. I need your assistance. I need a dedicated researcher to find out how the U.S. Navy was finally forced to admit Blacks into combat roles on warships, rather than restricting them to menial tasks."

"You want me to help you with your book?"

"In the process of completing your doctorate, yes."

This, I realized, was a classic case of "I'll scratch your back if you scratch mine." The tradeoff seemed fair. But I had a few questions.

"When I was in the raft… when I finally found the PC 1264, I'm sure I heard Gramps saying, nigger ship. But how could that be? He was already gone. Makes no sense."

"That characterization was discussed by me and your grandfather. Sadly, that's the way the ship's crew was viewed. It was, however, the key to our interest."

"But how could I know about that?"

"You were with your grandfather at the end?"

"For days."

"You seldom left the room?"

"Correct."

"When cogent, your grandfather spoke?"

"Right."

"About many things during an emotional time?"

"Yes, again."

"Then perhaps he used the words in question, but you somehow missed them. Your mind was perhaps elsewhere?"

"You want me to believe it all bubbled out of my unconscious?"

"It is possible."

"And finish the story?"

"As with the former…"

"I can't accept that."

"Then what are we left with, Garvey? Kansas, again!"

Fort Leavenworth, Kansas… and the 555th Parachute Infantry Company Monument. Back when I was a high school junior. Gramps and I had gone there to complete our research about America's first Black combat airborne unit. That's where I had heard the voice.

Garvey, I'm glad your grandfather brought you here… You would have made a fine member of the 555th. I'm glad we kicked in those doors so you could have a better life. Keep kicking them in for yourself and others. And don't forget us.

Gramps heard the voice too. But he didn't let on—at least, not at first. My unconscious at work? Projecting buried thoughts, dreams unrealized at the conscious level? Possible. But the voice was so clear.

And again at the Buffalo Soldiers Monument... another voice.

Glad to see you, Garvey. I was hoping you would come by... We'll remember your visit. And remember us. I'm not sure we always had the spirit, courage, and valor that you folks believe we had. We were just guys doing our best to keep the plains safe for settler and Native American alike. Wasn't easy.

"I never figured out what exactly happened in Kansas."

"Bordered on the mystical, Garvey."

"Gramps never really confirmed or denied the voices. By innuendo and poorly disguised body language, he conveyed two words to me."

"Which were?"

"Accept it."

"Might be a good thing to do, then as well as now."

What could I say? Mystical experiences are not easily bent and shaped into neat packages. They seemed to have a life of their own. They didn't dispute facts; they simply provided another way of experiencing reality. Acceptance, at least for the moment, seemed the best path to take. That said, I changed the subject.

"Gramps mentioned two ships—or at least, that's what I think I heard. But I only knew about the PC 1264. What's the other ship? And how are the two ships related? Does it have something to do with Black sailors?"

The questions flowed out of me. Professor Richmond merely smiled as he shifted his large body in his oversized chair.

"Garvey, my boy, I think you're trying to pull one over on your old professor. Asking questions to which you already have the answers."

"Me?" I said with a slight smile.

"You," he responded with a chuckle. "The photograph you showed your folks... the picture of the crew of the PC 1264. What was it you said to your mother?"

"They're all Black."

"And that's the connection, isn't it?"

"Two ships? Two Black crews?"

"Even Pearl the Wonder Dog would have figured that out, Garvey. Permit me to show you some photographs."

Showing the agility of a former athlete, he sprang from his chair to a file cabinet bursting with a career's worth of "don't throw away this stuff" carefully placed in ubiquitous files. From a rather thick folder, Professor Richmond pulled out a handful of photographs and placed them before me. As he did, he said, "I had to do a lot of digging to find these. It was almost like the Navy didn't want them made public but didn't have the gumption to destroy them. Perhaps it was because the Navy doesn't like to lose a ship... Or maybe, just maybe, the record of a fine crew, if completely expunged, would, for lack of a better way of saying it, amount to a mortal sin. At least for men who go down to the sea. Anyway, check out this photo."

I didn't recognize the ship in the photo. There was a good reason for this—it wasn't the PC 1264.

"That's the USS Mason (DE 529) at sea, August 1944, covered with a camouflage paint pattern."

THE OTHER SHIP

"Beautiful, isn't she? A destroyer escort... smaller than a destroyer but larger than a PC like the 1264. Her keel was laid in the Boston Naval Yard in October 1943, and she was commissioned on March 20, 1944. Her sponsor was Mrs. David Mason."

"Who?"

"The mother of Ensign Newton Henry Mason."

"Who?"

"Garvey, you're starting to sound like an owl. Ensign Mason was attached to Fighter Squadron Three aboard the Yorktown. He died following aerial combat against the Japanese during the Battle of the Coral Sea, May 8th and 9th, 1942. He was posthumously awarded the Distinguished Flying Cross for his courage and skill—for his, and I quote the citation, 'devotion to duty.'"

"This is the second ship?"

"Yes. Here's the first ship—your PC 1264. And here's her crew again. The ship's Black crew."

"Okay."

"And this," he said, sliding another photo across the desk, "is the Mason being launched in November 1943. You can clearly see her numbers—529—painted on the starboard side. Sliding into history... even before she knew her crew would be Black."

USS MASON (DE 529)

Professor Richmond, clearly enjoying himself, slid another photo across the desk. This one depicted sailors standing at attention—Black sailors, standing proud and disciplined.

"There you have it," he said, leaning back in his chair with a satisfied grin.

I studied the image, taking in the details. Two ships, two crews... Black crews... both in the US Navy at roughly the same time during the war. The connection was unmistakable.

Coincidence? The thought flickered in my mind, only to be quickly doused by an old adage I'd often heard from Gramps: "Don't believe in coincidences."

THE SECOND BLACK CREW

"And my last photograph, Garvey," the professor said, sliding a final image across the desk. "Taken in New York Harbor, sometime in 1944, before the crew went ashore for liberty."

I leaned forward as he added, "The Black crew, dressed in their Navy Blues, assembled proudly at the bow of the ship."

ON LIBERTY

"I'm convinced. Two ships... The PC 1264... And Gramps' other ship... The USS Mason (DE 529)... Each with a Black crew... One chasing Nazi subs... The other, I assume, escorting convoys across the unforgiving North Atlantic..."

"Garvey, your assumptions are 10-4."

"But why is this so important to you, Professor Richmond, and to Gramps? There must be something more."

"Garvey, I've read a Robert B. Parker book or two. As before, you already know the answer, just as Spenser, the strong-armed gent, generally does in his fictionalized existence."

"These are the 'nigger crews'?"

"Sadly, that's what many called them."

"You want to know how they—the crews—ended up on naval warships?"

"Your grandfather suspected a parallel experience to the men of the 555th Airborne with these Black sailors. He... Make that we... We wanted you to tell their story, too. You know, the Bluejackets kicking in 'old Jim Crow' at sea."

"We?"

"Gramps... Me... And now you... Partners all in this academic enterprise to dredge up the past... To understand what really happened and why..."

"Our goal?"

"It's already been said, Garvey. Finish the story."

CHAPTER 6

EVELYN

UNIVERSITY OF WASHINGTON LIBRAY

I stared at the computer. I had been staring at it for hours. And, of course, it stared back at me—a blank, black screen waiting for me to type a key, write a word, or provide some clue as to what I wanted. I could almost hear the Apple 7000 saying, somewhat belligerently:

"Look, pal, this staring business isn't getting us anywhere. Why not meet me halfway? If you want to access some information, type in a few lines. In other words, give me a break. I get frustrated too. My circuits only work when your fingers dazzle the keyboard. You know… Tap… Tap…"

I was tired. Not exhausted, just bone-weary. I had been at this research for days, delving into every resource I could think of to learn about the USS Mason and the PC 1264. And there was so much more than I originally thought.

It seemed like my life was hemmed in and circumscribed by a steady routine of attending my graduate seminar at UW, working on my doctorate—which really meant untangling how these two U.S. Navy ships ended up with Black crews—and teaching one seminar of my own.

The subject of my seminar? One unforgettable day during World War II: May 8, 1945, the day the war in Europe ended. That's right…

V-E Day. It was the day the killing ended. At least in Europe. The Pacific was another matter.

My social life, which had only been "so-so" during my undergraduate years, was now non-existent. Buried in the basement of the university library, I spent my days researching, almost entirely oblivious to the co-eds who wandered by occasionally or the attractive library helpers on work-study programs who sauntered past, aimlessly doing whatever it was they did. Ego aside (as much as that's possible), every now and then a female student would sit across from me and try to catch my eye. Of course, I liked that. What guy wouldn't? But it takes two to play that game. All too often, I didn't respond in kind. You know… light flirtation… an engaging smile… the possibility of a date.

That was, until yesterday, when—surprisingly—the latest female incarnation appeared as if out of nowhere.

"Nice day, isn't it?" she asked.

"Hard to tell in this bunker," I responded, barely looking at her.

"You're a student here?"

"Sort of."

"Meaning?"

"Working on my doctoral thesis," I said, this time glancing more directly at this uninvited intruder into my life. I had to admit it—she was worth glancing at.

"You also teach?"

"Teaching a seminar. But how did you know?"

There was no direct answer. My attractive nemesis just shrugged her shoulders, saying, "I must have picked that up somewhere."

I nodded in turn. That was me, it seemed—an equal-opportunity uncommunicative conversationalist. However, I did avoid saying, "I also stare at my computer, especially when my brain goes dead."

"Doctoral candidate... teaching... taking classes. Wow. Big load. Makes my junior year look easy."

"Things are relative."

"You're a history major?"

"That's what they tell me. But how did you know?"

"Guessed. Of course, all those history books are suggestive."

"It would seem so. You?"

"Me? What?"

"Major?"

"Anthropology."

"I guess you dig your classes."

"That line is so old."

That was true. Old and stupid—certainly an unnecessary response to my surprising nervousness around this person. Fortunately, I avoided saying, "Into pots and bones, and spearheads?" And naturally, I didn't refer to her professors as "old fossils." Instead, I stifled the thought and remained quiet as an Egyptian mummy.

A long moment passed. It felt like an eternity to me.

"You ever get out of here?" she asked rather directly. "You know, take the stairs to the surface?"

"Not often enough."

"You should. Great football team this year. The Huskies could win it all."

"That's nice."

"Big supporter of the team, I see."

One shoulder moved involuntarily, suggesting either indifference or ignorance. My visitor's response caught me off guard.

"And do you have a name?"

"Garvey."

"That's it?"

"Garvey Morgan Langston."

"Nice to meet you."

I nodded again. My all-purpose response when the English language deserted me.

"A man of few words."

I resisted the temptation to nod again. Instead, I just stared straight ahead. Let me amend that—I stared at the young woman. I wasn't distracted. She was easy to stare at. She was so beautiful. Tall with a striking Polynesian look, her dark hair pulled tightly back, almost painfully so from my perch. Her flashing eyes were deep pools, dark and inviting. And the rest of her? So very attractive, slim and curving.

Then came the pitch.

"Going to the dance tonight, Garvey?"

"Dance?"

"Homecoming. Starts at 9:00 p.m. in the Campus Social Hall. Nostalgia music… The Beatles…"

I had to admit it—her pitch struck a responsive chord. This co-ed was a Beatles fan, as was my dad. In high school, he had covered his room with every bit of Beatlemania he could get his hands on—posters, pictures, a Beatles clock, and lots of books on the English invaders. He even painted his telephone to commemorate *Sgt. Pepper's Lonely Hearts Club Band*. When wall space proved inadequate, he'd plastered the ceiling with posters.

THE BEATLES

I was not immune to my dad's obsession. By force of parental control over the car CD player, I learned all the songs as he drove me around. It was a light form of child abuse, which turned out okay in the end.

"All You Need Is Love."

"What?"

"Just a Beatles song I recall."

"Great song."

"Not a bad message for the world."

"You're an idealist."

"Just a wayward romantic, Miss…"

And then she gave me her name. "Evelyn… Evelyn Maria Hernandez."

"Nice name."

"Actually, two or three names longer."

I smiled and remained silent.

Getting up, this interloper in my life, with only a hint of a smile and a wistful glance, said, "I'll look for you at the dance. You can't stay in this place forever."

And then she was gone.

Needless to say, I didn't go to the dance. But I should have. Don't ask me why I didn't; I'd only make up some foolish excuse. I thought about that pretty junior now and then over the next few days. Perhaps,

I thought, she'd wander into my life again. More to the point, I found myself hoping she would. And that, for me, was a first.

CHAPTER 7

CAMP ROBERT SMALLS

Back to another reality... I continued to stare at the computer screen. Though it was dark now, blank to the world, it had completed its task, which was to extend my mind beyond the reaches of UW into the archives of Yale, UCLA, and Georgia Tech, as well as the VA record repository in St. Louis and, of course, the Naval Academy in Annapolis. I might not have been connected to a dance date, but I was certainly linked to rich mines of information across the country.

All I had to do was go "tap, tap."

I had come across the name quite by accident. Fortuitously would best describe this break. Believe it or not, sometimes things happen just that way when you're researching. You just get lucky.

I had been trying to figure out where the Black sailors were trained before boarding the Mason or the PC 1264. Surely, there had to be a fort, some military camp, naval base, or university dormitory where they received basic training. But where? That was the question. It was as if this information was cloaked in secrecy.

And I was right.

Not only the training location but also the decision to launch a program for Black sailors in the first place was made quietly, behind the scenes. The decision to do this was not made by accident, nor was it met with joyous intention. But it had been made, as I would learn, by the Navy—quietly and in an effort to avoid public scrutiny.

It began with a simple administrative order of the day.

The Navy decided to open its ranks to general Black enlistment on June 1, 1942. The inductees would be trained at the Great Lakes Naval Training Center in Illinois. This was where thousands of young men from every creed, race, and ethnic background were being brought by the Navy to prepare for fighting a two-ocean war. This was where former shoe salesmen, truck drivers, and thrifty bankers learned the specialties and skills of naval warfare, often referred to as "ratings."

This was also true for the Black sailors, but they were housed and trained in a segregated camp within the Great Lakes Training Facility.

Pursuant to an order signed on April 21, 1942, by Secretary of the Navy Frank Knox, Camp Robert Smalls was established at the Great Lakes Naval Training Center. Its purpose was to provide a dedicated facility for "training Negro seamen at a time when the U.S. Navy was still segregated by race."

SEGREGATED CAMP ROBERT SMALLS

The Navy, I found out, was not particularly happy about this. The President had to be pushed hard by Black politicians, civil rights leaders, and Black businesspeople to take action. FDR, always mindful of the Black vote, reluctantly and quietly responded to the pressure. More on this in time... The Navy would follow the example of the Army and its experiment with Black paratroopers. Train them. Provide actual combat training. Severely scrutinize their behavior under combat conditions. Reach an unbiased conclusion as to their readiness for combat. If successful, recommend their inclusion on a limited basis at first. In time, take steps to desegregate the Navy so that Black sailors might someday hear the words that too often bypassed them: "Man your battle stations."

Even as I learned all this, I was troubled... I called out, "Gramps, wish you were here. We need to talk."

"Gramps, this is crazy," I found myself saying. "Asking young men to train for war in a near Jim Crow situation."

"What did you expect, Garvey? Bombs bursting over Pearl Harbor were not going to erase 100 years of social segregation in Alabama and Mississippi... Get real. Prejudice, irrational biases, and discrimination, whether on a bus..."

"Sit in the back in the Black section…"

"Or in a cafeteria…"

"This section is reserved for whites…"

"And at the voting booth…"

"Read this document to prove your right to vote…"

"Garvey, it's nice to know you're up on bigotry."

"But, Gramps, the Great Lakes Training Center was in Illinois… Land of Lincoln…"

"Well, that's the thing about prejudice… It doesn't discriminate. I've always loved that line. Conveys so much with so few words."

"But we were in a war against Nazi Germany's racist attitudes toward Jews and others."

"We were, weren't we?"

"You tell me."

Making headway, I thought. I now knew where the men were trained. I didn't, however, know why Secretary Knox finally issued the order to train Black enlistees. Was the White House pushing him? Or was it the Negro press? The manpower needs of war? Or was it the 1942 mid-term congressional elections? Probably all of these factors… Of course, one reason was never stated. It was simply the right thing to do.

Camp Robert Smalls… Why was a segregated facility operating at a time when the Navy was opening its ranks to all Americans? Were the men being trained for the PC 1264 and the USS Mason even before the construction of these ships? Lots of questions…

I decided to sidestep most of these questions, at least for a while… But curiosity had gotten the better of me on another matter. I decided to find out something about Robert Smalls. Who was this person? Why was a camp named after him? Little did I know, my research would lead me into a world of irony and paradox, wrapped up in a package of fickleness and surprises, if one can speak of history in that manner.

ROBERT SMALLS

Surprisingly, Robert Smalls was a ship's pilot and sea captain prior to the American Civil War. Early in the conflict, he secretly commandeered a Confederate transport ship, the CSS Planter, in Charleston Harbor and sailed it past Southern guns to escape to the Federal ships blockading the port. History records that he made it, sailing smoothly past Confederate fortifications to freedom. No Underground Railroad for this seafaring man.

CSS PLANTER

It should be noted that Smalls was a Negro slave.

Smalls was a Charleston Harbor pilot, though, as property, he was never given that title. On May 12, 1862, he was aboard the armed Confederate military transport, the CSS Planter, when the ship's white officers went ashore. Smalls recognized his chance. Along with seven other enslaved crewmen, Smalls decided to take over the ship and make a run for the Union ships maintaining the blockade. Along the way, he picked up his family and the relatives of other crewmen and then began his daring escape. One gets the sense that Smalls had thought this out well in advance of his opportunity. Good planning never hurts.

Though the odds were against him, Smalls made it, providing the Union with a treasure trove of useful information, including a codebook that revealed Confederate secret ship signals and the placement of mines and torpedoes in Charleston Harbor. He also brought with him a cargo of valuable artillery pieces. And Smalls himself had detailed knowledge of Charleston Harbor's defenses.

He became an instant hero in the North, where Congress awarded him $1,500 for the CSS Planter, a huge sum in that day. Moreover, he achieved a degree of celebrity status. He also met with President Lincoln and passionately pushed him to include Northern Blacks and Southern runaway slaves in the Union military. He continued this persuasion with Edwin Stanton, the Secretary of War. Ultimately, Smalls' arguments would carry weight with both the President and the Secretary. It should be noted that Smalls served with the Union army as a civilian. He also participated in 17 different military engagements while fighting for the Union. Without question, he was a man of words and actions.

In December 1863, Smalls became the first Black captain of a vessel in the service of the United States. He was appointed captain of the USS Planter, now a Union transport ship. In April 1865, along with other warships, he captained the former Confederate vessel into Charleston Harbor to raise the American flag over recaptured Fort Sumter. How's that for irony, with a bit of revenge thrown in?

During the Reconstruction period following the Civil War, Smalls was elected several times from the 7th district of South Carolina between 1884 and 1889. He was a member of the 44th, 45th, and the 47th through the 49th U.S. Congresses. While in the House of Representatives, he introduced an amendment to a bill to reduce and restructure the United States Army. His amendment stated, "Hereafter in the enlistment of men in the Army... no distinction whatsoever shall be made on account of race or color." Sadly, Congress did not take up the amendment for consideration. It languished in committee and died. And with it, an opportunity to change American history...

The Civil War, Smalls understood in time, had been fought to free the slave and protect the Union. The war had not been fought to guarantee the former slave total equality in every aspect of national life. As for the armed forces, it would be almost eighty years before the issue would be settled with President Harry S. Truman's decision to desegregate the country's military in 1948. Somewhere in Charleston Harbor, aboard the USS Planter, Robert Smalls was applauding.

With the eclipse of military-enforced Republican control in the South in 1876 and the onslaught of Jim Crow laws, Black Codes, and rampant government-supported discrimination, the accomplishments and heroics of Blacks in the Civil War were pushed aside, condemned to the trash bin of history. Forgotten were the 186,097 Blacks in 163 Army units who served courageously during the war, and the hundreds more who served honorably in the Navy. Forgotten was the heroic role of Robert Smalls.

In place of the facts of history, a disturbing view took hold. No, make that an unreasoning understanding, perpetuated by white Southerners and others opposed to the advancement of the former slave. Essentially, the view said:

White men will:

never accept the Negro in a position of authority over them.
always consider themselves to be a superior race.
necessarily consider Blacks, therefore, to be members of an inferior race.
never accept the Black as an equal.
always refuse to accept intimacies between the races.

SERVING THEIR COUNTRY

The Navy's view was summed up in 1941, just days after Pearl Harbor, by the Secretary of War, Frank Knox:

"Mingling Negroes with whites in the relatively large numbers of non-rated billets on larger ships would inevitably promote race friction and lowered efficiency."

Knox's logic here was simple: keep the races separated in order to maintain the fighting morale of the services.

This lack of enthusiasm for Black sailors was attributed by some naval officers to the "Negro's relative unfamiliarity with the sea or the large inland lakes, and their consequent fear of water." It should be noted that no empirical data supported this claim, and naturally, this view was not extended to white inductees.

Still another avenue of resistance to Black sailors was naval reliance on Gresham's Law, which, when stated in popular terms, suggested "bad money drives out good money." Used by the Navy, Sir Thomas Gresham's sixteenth-century law ran counter to universal conscription, or the forced integration of the service. Bad money in this case was the Black sailor. Good money was the white sailor.

Stated in another manner, the Navy and the Marines in particular, prior to World War II, prided themselves on being all-voluntary services, where only the best men were accepted. Lowered standards or skills of drafted enlistees, it was thought, would infect the whole establishment, thereby lowering the efficiency of the Navy and the Marines. In particular, forced desegregation of the Navy would only heighten and exaggerate this process.

In a letter written in 1940, the Secretary of the Navy, Frank Knox, explained and justified these views. He was writing to Charles Poletti, the Lieutenant Governor of New York State.

"Experience of many years in the Navy has shown clearly that men of the colored race in any other branch than the Mess-man Branch, and promoted to the position of petty officer, cannot maintain discipline among men of the white race over whom they may be placed by reason of their rating. As a result, teamwork, harmony, and ship efficiency are seriously handicapped."

This was the stereotypical view that led to these statistics in late 1943. Over 98% of the Navy was white. Only 26,909 Blacks were in the Navy, a figure that would rise as the war continued. At the time, over 9,200 Black sailors were stewards. Over 2,000 Blacks were with the Seabees. More than 6,600 were in the general services with little hope of gaining ratings.

"Gramps, you there?"

"What's on your mind, Garvey?"

"Stupidity."

"Knox's views?"

"Yeah."

"How could the country accept such bunk? Especially the Navy?"

"Good management practice? Efficiency? Higher performance in the deadly arts of war?"

"You don't believe that, Gramps."

"Not about me. These views were held by a majority of Americans in the decades following the Emancipation Proclamation."

"Down to Pearl Harbor."

"For some, even to today."

"Hard to believe it."

"Believe it. Stereotypes are difficult to eliminate. Hell, it was believed that the Japanese had a congenital trait of myopia, making it impossible for them to fly airplanes with any precision. That stereotype crumbled in Hawaii with the sinking of the USS Arizona."

"Blacks were linked with Japs as people who couldn't do things?"

"Crudely put, but yes. You have evidence to the contrary in the file Professor Richmond gave you."

"The documents?"

"The photographs… The almost forgotten photographs… Take a good look at them. A picture is worth a thousand words. They dispel all the shopworn prejudices that inhibited desegregating the armed forces."

How did Gramps know about this file and the photographs? I couldn't get the question out of my head. Was Gramps privy to everything I was doing? But how could that be? Or was I carrying on an internal conversation with myself? The possibility existed. Or still, what was it Gramps had once said? "Garvey, my boy. I'll always be with you. Just keep that in mind."

Back to the photographs… I took Gramps' suggestion to heart. I checked out the photographs.

Gramps was right. The photographs contradicted a century of misplaced values and an unappreciated people.

The first photograph showed gunner's mates from the USS Mason receiving training on a 20 mm gun in January 1944. They were learning all aspects of using and maintaining the weapon.

The second photograph showed members of the Mason's Black crew receiving compass training, again in January 1944.

The third photo was taken aboard the PC 1264, where members of the crew were practicing with a "blinks lamp" to earn their signalman's rating.

The last photograph depicted members of the USS Mason receiving navigation training, again from January 1944.

It was apparent from the photographs that, when appropriate instruction was provided to Black sailors by competent instructors, their progress was equal to any group in the Navy, despite biased views and prejudicial attitudes to the contrary. All that was needed was an unbiased opportunity.

"Gramps…"

"Don't say it. Inferior people can't learn the arts of a modern warship."

"The photographs dispute that."

"Don't they?"

"I keep thinking I've missed something."

"Keep checking in the file, Garvey. You never know what you'll come across."

"Leading me on, aren't you?"

"Me? A dead man?"

"You're in my head."

"Your mind, Garvey… Not enough room in your head."

"Very funny."

"Well, it's your joke."

"Gramps…"

There was no response, as I could hear from Gramps. Of course, a non-verbal shrug or smile is difficult to convey in words, especially when the "living" are, it seems, listening to the deceased. You just sense it. Somewhere, I knew with absolute certainty that Gramps had a wrinkled grin on his face and was about to drop another clue on me.

CHAPTER 8

OHIO

My rapt thoughts were interrupted. My computer screen was blinking. For the life of me, I couldn't remember tapping any keys. But there was no doubt... Four letters were appearing on the screen, blinking repetitively, again and again --- OHIO, OHIO, OHIO. What the heck was going on? Crazy as it sounds, nothing happened even when I tried to end the message. The same message just kept blinking... I felt like strangling Yahoo or laser-beaming Google. No matter what I did, the blinking continued. It was like Stephen King was alive in my computer. Or maybe Edgar Allan Poe... I was getting desperate. Fatigue was overwhelming my good sense. Only one avenue seemed open to me: pull the plug on the infernal contraption. I reached for the plug and was about to yank it when...

"Garvey, I wouldn't do that."

"Gramps?"

"You were expecting someone else?"

"I need to take care of something."

"Correct. But not that."

"You're at it again. Controlling, manipulating."

"How about assisting?"

"Okay, assist."

"I already did."

"What?"

"Check the screen."

"OHIO!"

"Figure it out."

Gramps had me again. What was he up to? A clue, yes... OHIO... A mid-west state... The Buckeyes... So what? How could OHIO be related to the subject at hand? Black sailors... The USS Mason... The PC1264... What was the connection?

Something, I knew, was needed to break the logjam... Something to change the Navy's attitude about Black seamen... The Japanese attack... A possibility... Our declaration of war... Manpower needs... Volunteers... Conscription...

The draft... 1941... Something about OHIO... Overheated, my mind kept grasping for an elusive thought. What was it?

Could OHIO be an acronym? Angry soldiers... No, angry draftees... Soldiers threatening desertion... The first national draft in peacetime... 1940... FDR signs the law...

Hitler was devouring Europe... Tokyo was at war in China and coveting Southeast Asia... Late in 1941... Fearful of Berlin and Tokyo, the President acted... The Selective Service Act was modified. The twelve-month tour of military duty was extended by six months because of international crises...

The acronym… Finally… "Over the Hill in October…" That was it. Had to be…

American soldiers were threatening to leave the Army when their original one-year tour of duty was over in October… Demonstrations about the extension… Parents crying foul… Businesses complaining… Families upset… Then the Japanese attack… Congress acted… The Selective Service Act was extended from six months to the end of the war. In other words, indefinite terms of service…

That was it. There was a manpower crisis. The domestic economy needed workers, especially as the country geared up for war. But the military also needed men. Ultimately, by the millions… Manpower shortages loomed. Something had to be done. Only two groups were underutilized --- women and Blacks.

Something in the Selective Service Act about them, at least indirectly… But what was it?

My fingers danced on the computer keyboard. To my astonishment, the computer responded. A whirl of tapping… Seconds later, the screen brightened with the past.

President Roosevelt signed the controversial Selective Training and Service Act on September 16, 1940. This was the first conscription act in the United States during a time of peace. Young men would be drafted in great numbers, as opposed to individuals volunteering. This was not the first time conscription had been used by the government. In 1861, during the Civil War, men from both the Union and the Confederacy were required to join their respective armies. Again, conscription was used during World War I to bolster the armed forces.

THE DRAFT

The Act, also known as the Burke-Wadsworth Act, required that all male citizens between the ages of 21 and 45 register for the draft. Individual names would be drawn by a lottery system. Initially, the Act limited the number of men to be trained to 900,000, with exceptions made for conscientious objectors. The term of service was twelve months, but this point was changed after the Japanese attack. The period of service was extended until the war's end.

The Act specifically provided that:

Any person, regardless of race or color, between the ages of eighteen and fifty-five, shall be afforded an opportunity to volunteer for induction into the land and naval forces of the United States for the training and service prescribed in sub-section B...

The preamble to this section read:

"The Congress further declares that in a free society the obligations and privileges of military training and service should be shared generally in accordance with a fair and just system of selective compulsory military training and service."

The Act further stated, "... There shall be no discrimination against any person on account of race or color."

That was it. That was the connection.

On paper, at least, America would fight the Axis Powers with an armed force in which every citizen had an opportunity to participate and advance in position or rating based on his intelligence, skill, and bravery. No racial distinctions… No Jim Crow in the military… On paper, at least… This, at last, was the basis for a color-free military and, most particularly, a Navy that accepted and promoted Black seamen.

All that was necessary was for the Navy to agree.

CHAPTER 9

THE MEETING

U.S. NAVAL ACADEMY – FEBRUARY 2036

The Academy was established in 1845 under the Secretary of the Navy, George Bancroft, on a 338-acre site, where once Fort Severn stood at the confluence of the Severn River and the Chesapeake Bay. Each year, the Academy, which is a National Historic Landmark, graduated about 1,000 midshipmen, who were commissioned into the Navy as ensigns or as second lieutenants in the Marine Corps. In other words, the Academy churns out officers.

And, today, I was there to meet one.

I couldn't help but marvel at the historical weight of the place as I made my way through its iron gates. The cobblestone streets, the majestic buildings with their classical facades, and the imposing naval insignias on every corner seemed to whisper stories of men who had walked these paths before me—men whose names were etched into the annals of history, whose journeys and sacrifices shaped the very core of the Navy.

But I wasn't here for a history lesson. I was here because, somehow, in the course of my research into the naval history surrounding the WWII-era ships, I had stumbled upon a name that stood out. A name tied to the wrecks I had been studying—the name of an officer who might have been on board the PC 1217, one of the ships I had unearthed in my work. I had to know more.

The man I was about to meet had written a letter to me after hearing about my dissertation. He claimed to have information that could fill the gaps in my research. And now, I was on my way to meet him.

The letter was brief, cryptic even, but the promise of what it might contain was enough to compel me to make the trip. I'd already spent so many years buried in the archives, pouring over microfilm and yellowed documents, but this could be different. This could be the connection that would tie everything together. The missing piece to the puzzle.

I reached the Academy's visitor center, where I was told to wait for my contact. As I sat in the cool lobby, I couldn't shake the feeling that this meeting—this day—would be the beginning of something much bigger. The kind of story I had been chasing for years. And, just maybe, it would lead me closer to uncovering the truth about my own family's history within the Navy.

GRADUATING NAVAL OFFICERS

My interest in the Academy, which I reached by rental car, was the Chester W. Nimitz Library, and most particularly, the William W. Jeffries Memorial Archives. There I was to meet Captain Zack Patterson, retired. Professor Richmond had provided the name and scheduled the meeting. Apparently, they were chums based on their abiding love of American naval history.

At first, I had been reluctant to make the trip. A sort of library dungeon inertia had a strong grip on me. I was too glued to my chair in front of that darn computer. I had to be pushed a bit.

"I know it's a long trip, Garvey, but it's worth it."

"Professor, he can't just send me the files?"

"Some perhaps…"

"But…"

"He's an old guy, mid-80's, I believe, and he's not really into computer attachments and all that kind of thing. He's a face-to-face sort of guy. He needs to look you in the eye."

"Still…"

"Garvey, he wants to meet you. What did he say? 'Any plebe with the guts to row around that graveyard in a dinky rubber raft is my kind of sailor.'"

"Plebe?"

"It's an abbreviation of the Ancient Roman word plebian, and what newly accepted candidates to the Academy are called."

"His kind of sailor, huh?"

"Or he wouldn't send for you."

I had no choice. I liked the pat on the back, and I needed to see Captain Zach Patterson. His father had worked in the Special Programs Unit (SPU) back in the 1940's, and that group was key to understanding how Black seamen ended up on the USS Mason and the PC 1264, based on my research to this point. The aging captain was a living resource. He had "insider information," which I needed. And, of course, Professor Richmond was right. Some things are better shared face to face. I guess it adds the human element. Facts, you might say, with emotions and motivations, not merely digital bits floating through the air, oblivious to their significance.

After passing through security and entering the Academy grounds, I got directions to where we were meeting—the Tripoli Monument. I had been told to be there by 1300. I was there on time—1:00 p.m. I didn't want to be AWOL on this visit.

THE MONUMENT

The suspense of Garvey's meeting with Captain Patterson intensifies as they finally dive into the heart of Garvey's research. Here's how this pivotal moment could unfold:

Standing by the monument was a slim, ramrod-straight older man with a mop of brilliant white hair combed carefully back, contrasting sharply with his deeply tanned face. He wore gray trousers and a dark blue double-breasted blazer, complemented by highly polished black navy shoes and a flame red tie. Considering my somewhat slovenly appearance— a tired corduroy jacket, wrinkled tan shirt, and pants badly in need of a pressing, plus my scuffed shoes—I feared the retired Captain might just throw me in the brig.

I screwed up my courage, straightened my back, and walked over, my arm extended for the hearty handshake I was sure was coming. I just hoped it wouldn't hurt too much.

"Captain Patterson?"

"You're Garvey?"

"Yes."

"You took a flimsy rubber raft into that God-forsaken graveyard?"

"I'm afraid so."

"Damn! You don't look like a pirate."

"Me? Blackbeard? Long John Silver? You're right."

"No Navy Seal training? Not involved in special operations?"

"Only at the movies."

"Son, the Navy could use you."

"Can't swim well."

"We'll put three flotation jackets on you."

Okay, I'll admit it. I couldn't help it. I grinned from proverbial ear to ear. Another pat on the back… So much better than the brig or walking the plank…

"Let's have a seat, Garvey."

With a hearty smile, the old man shunted me to a bench adjacent to the monument. Before I could apologize for my less-than-Esquire Magazine look, or ask about the Black crews, Captain Patterson puffed out his chest, as if he were on the bridge of an attacking destroyer, brooking no interruption. "Let me tell you about this spot."

I acquiesced.

"Garvey, believe it or not, this is the oldest military monument in the United States. Not many people know that. A bit of trivia, right?" He gestured to the imposing structure. "It honors our naval heroes of the First Barbary Coast War, 1801–1805. Ever hear of it?"

"Something about fighting the Barbary States… Muslim states in Algeria and Morocco."

"Know your history, I see… Professor Richmond said you were up on things."

"Jefferson wouldn't pay the high tributes demanded by the Sultanate of Morocco for American ships to sail without fear of an attack in the Mediterranean. Weren't American ships being seized and the crews held for large ransoms?"

"Succinctly put and yes. A bunch of pirates preying on our seamen… Led to our first declared war fought on foreign soil. Gave us our first post-Revolution heroes—Master Commandant Richard Somers, Lieutenant James Caldwell, and James Decatur, the brother of Stephen Decatur. Quite a group…"

"And our first war with an Arab country."

"Given our recent history, a thoughtful comment, young man."

I shrugged.

"Very thoughtful indeed," Captain Patterson repeated.

"And the monument, Sir?"

"Carved in Livorno, Italy in 1806. Brought to the United States on the USS Constitution, and then it began its travels. Thirty feet high column with an eagle on top… The whole monument is mounted on an elaborate base adorned with allegorical figures representing Glory, Fame, History, and Commerce. Quite a chunk of marble… Designed by Giovanni C. Micali… He added a nice inscription."

"As a small tribute of respect to their memory and of admiration of their valor so worthy of imitation their brother officers have erected this monument."

That inscription, I thought to myself, might have been applied to the 555th Parachute unit. Probably to the two navy crews I had crossed the country to learn about. Maybe that's what Captain Patterson was inferring by our visit to the monument.

"The monument was brought directly to Annapolis?" I asked, breaking from my musings.

"I'm afraid not. In 1806, it was installed in the old Washington Navy Yard. Two years later, it was moved to the west terrace of the Capitol. Finally got here in 1860."

"And stayed."

"Until now, anyway…"

"It is striking. I've never seen anything like it."

"Always good to add to our life experience, Garvey. But you're here to learn about something else… The Special Programs Unit…"

I nodded. I feigned coolness. Inside, I was churning. Truthfully, I was impatient. I was prepared to fight the Barbary pirates single-handedly if that would get the Captain going. It turned out I didn't have to.

"Garvey, you want to know about the super-secret organization my father was attached to during the big war? You want to know about its secrets?"

"Yes. At least as it relates to all-Black U.S. Navy crews."

"The USS Mason?"

"Yes."

"The 1264?"

"Affirmative, Sir."

CHAPTER 10

PRESSURE

"Garvey, my father was wounded during the Guadalcanal Campaign in '42. What I'm about to tell you was conveyed to me by him and through my own research. My father lost a leg when the Japanese came down the 'slot' during the Battle of Cape Esperance. He was on the USS Duncan, a destroyer. The ship took one in the gut. So did my old man. The Navy gave him a desk job after he healed. Eventually, he was placed in the new Planning and Control Division the Navy established after Pearl Harbor. From there, as it turned out, he was assigned to the Special Unit team."

"Your father was lucky to survive."

"We called him Long John Silver in our family."

"He had a sense of humor, I take it?"

"Got him through lots of stuff. Now back to what you flew across the states to hear—the 'guinea pigs' and the woman behind the scenes."

Guinea pigs... A woman... What could they possibly have to do with Black sailors, I thought? I really needed help with that one.

"Remember, little was done before Pearl Harbor to treat Black seamen in a fair and just manner. Too much racism in the Navy... After the attack, the NAACP requested that the Navy give serious consideration to how best to utilize the services of Black sailors. That request went to Secretary Knox. Basically, the question before Knox boiled down to this: would the Navy now, because of the increased need for recruits, accept Negroes for more than just mass-man duty?" In short, would these men be trained for combat duty? The question went right to the heart of the matter.

"The Navy's unequivocal answer was that there would be 'no change in existing policy.' Naval policy would remain unchanged. Circumstances may have changed at Pearl Harbor, but not the tradition-bound Navy.

"This unsatisfactory response led to a direct appeal to President Roosevelt and, indirectly, to his wife, Eleanor. Roosevelt sent the NAACP's appeal on to Mark Ethridge, the chairman of the Fair Employment Practices Committee (FEPC), which had been created by Executive Order 8802. The mission of the FEPC was to ensure that there was 'no discrimination in the employment of workers in the defense industries or government because of race, creed, color, or national origin.' This effort was due in large part to A. Philip Randolph, who, as the founding president of the Brotherhood of Sleeping Car Porters, urged the government to assist Negroes.

"Roosevelt created the FEPC to quell demands for equality. Unfortunately, the agency was given little power to regulate employment practices. It could preach, but it couldn't enforce. A small budget and modest personnel meant there could be little real enforcement—no teeth. Some historians believe it was set up as a political necessity, yet doomed to fail. Racism also played a role in its ineffectiveness. In the South, politicians staunchly refused to cooperate with the FEPC. Angry white workers did not want equality of opportunity. They wanted jobs and the best pay possible. Blacks could have what was left over.

"So you had political interests... Economic interests... Societal interests... And, of course, the interests of the Navy...

"Ethridge, however, did make a good faith effort. He met with the Navy's General Board, which was charged with formulating Navy policy."

"Sounds like a good guy."

"He was. On the sidelines, Mrs. Roosevelt watched. She had a keen interest in dealing with what many called the 'Negro problem.' Her intentions were straightforward: all citizens should be given the same opportunity to improve themselves. She also had the ear of the President.

"In time, Ethridge reported back to the President with unfavorable news. First, the Fair Practices Committee had no authority over the Navy, particularly where race was concerned. The best the Navy would do, if required, was to place Blacks on small ships in the Caribbean or on harbor crafts, but not necessarily outside of the kitchen. The President, however, would have to order the Navy to do so. The Navy would not act unless forced. The President responded with a note to the Bureau of Navigation (BUNAV) stating:

'I think that with all the Navy activities, BUNAV might invent something that colored enlistees could do in addition to the rating of mess-man.'

"The ball was back in the General Board's court; that is, BUNAV. After considerable discussion, the Board replied with a singular either/or recommendation: '... either Negroes be enlisted in the mess-man branch or, if this proved not feasible, for general service.' If general service were the option taken by the government, units would be segregated. Blacks might be in combat roles, but equally so, segregated from whites. The Board argued that integration wouldn't work. The Board stated:

'Discrimination is but part and parcel of similar discrimination throughout the United States, not only against the Negro, but in the Pacific States and in Hawaii against citizens of Asiatic descent.'

"The situation, the Board concluded, wasn't very democratic, but it was reality. General service would be provided but, if integration wouldn't work, how could you properly segregate aboard a ship?"

"That's a tough one, Captain Patterson. A real Catch-22."

"Extremely so. Especially for professional officers on the Board, who were guided by precepts of honor and integrity, and who were dedicated to the defense of their country... For them, nothing could take precedence over fighting the war in the most efficient manner."

"Their personal views?"

"Of no real consequence... The world was a bloody mess. Someone was going to lose. They didn't want it to be America. Germany, yes... Japan, yes... America, no... As a group, the Board felt that to experiment with fixed social customs and folkways would only create problems for the Navy, therefore disrupting Naval efficiency needed to win the war."

"Mess-man for a Black man or segregated general service... Not much of a choice."

"Life is not perfect, Garvey. The Board saw segregation as an essential principle of naval administration."

"The General Board recognizes, and appreciates, the social and economic problems involved, and has striven to reconcile these requirements with what it feels must be paramount in any consideration, namely the maintenance at the highest level of fighting efficiency in the Navy."

"Always efficiency, Captain."

"Winning a war is not about resolving all the ills of society. Men die in war. Efficiency reduces the dead. Your dead."

"Ugly equation."

"But true with mathematical precision."

"Still ugly."

"Talk to a Gold Star Mother. See what she thinks."

"All this put the President in a box."

"The Board gave Roosevelt a qualifier, saying:"

The Navy, if so ordered, would institute Negro units with the least disadvantage, as in naval shore establishments, small local defense vessels of naval districts, or in some construction units and composite Marine battalions, and possibly some selected Coast Guard cutters."

"It was now up to the President, Captain?"

"Indeed."

"A lot of weight on his shoulders."

"Especially when your wife was pushing."

"As all this was happening, the NAACP reached out to the first lady. The organization saw the war needs as an opportunity, saying with emphasis:

'If our sons are going to fight for freedom abroad, then we expect some attention to be paid to our struggles here at home.'"

Mrs. Roosevelt agreed. She became the liaison for Blacks with the power structure in Washington—the White House, the Congress, and the Pentagon. In doing so, she risked vilification for her support of equality and justice for all in the military services. It was not uncommon for the Oval Office to receive hundreds of angry calls when Mrs. Roosevelt spoke out. On one occasion, just the rumor that she would ride in an open car with a Black woman stirred protests in Georgia."

"Hard to believe."

THE FIRST LADY

"Believe it, Garvey. America had powerful racial attitudes, which she was running up against. She was accused of meddling—an unelected woman who had not been appointed to any governmental position. With her husband, she was charged with wanting to appease Negro politicians who were trying to get the army to commit to Negro officers."

"But Roosevelt did want Negro votes."

"Absolutely, Garvey. That vote helped him win a difficult third-term election against Wendell Wilkie in 1940. He needed that vote in the upcoming '42 Congressional elections. No question about it. But he also wanted to do something for the Black draftee. The anger, however, was palpable, especially when Mrs. Roosevelt went public, suggesting strongly that the fairness provision of the Selective Service Act should be implemented."

"I'm picking up on some irony here, Captain."

"Fire away."

"First, the Navy wanted the Black recruits for essentially custodial services in order to fight racist regimes, yet was unwilling to provide such recruits with the same combat opportunities as whites. And second, white inductees were at risk partially because Blacks were not permitted to be in combat units. Finally, more whites had to be called up due to the loss of others in battle, while leaving many physically capable Blacks undrafted or, if drafted, not in combat units. Talk about a crazy situation. And illogical… Whites are more at risk because Blacks aren't in combat positions, but whites refuse to work with Blacks in combat situations, thereby making it difficult to reduce the risk factors for whites."

"Bravo. You hit the nail on the head. Three times, I might add."

"Well, that brings us to the key question, Sir. What did the President decide?"

"He pushed the Navy. On April 7, 1942, the Navy announced that beginning on June 1st, Negroes could enlist for general service as well as in the mess-man branch. Mrs. Roosevelt cheered the Navy on, even though editorials around the country referred to the decision as 'Eleanor's Folly.'"

"And this was before the USS Mason and the PC 1264 were built."

"They weren't even on the drawing boards. Two years would pass before these ships became a reality."

"Crews were being trained for ships not yet built. Hard to believe… And during those two years?"

"My father would be hard at work, Garvey."

CHAPTER 11

SPECIAL PROGRAM UNIT

The Captain excused himself. He needed to meet with an old friend for a few minutes. He would catch up with me in the Nimitz Library, history section, on the third floor of the building. As I walked over to the library, I muttered to myself, "I sure wish you were here, Gramps. You'd love this place. Tradition... Honor... Duty... Things we seldom talk about anymore. Here, those intangibles are tangible, manifest, meaningful... I like the focus too. Defend the country against her enemies. Real clarity. No if's, or but's... Not like our general society where so many things are complicated, contentious, and so very partisan. Here, it's simple, if not deadly. Nuances be damned. When in harm's way, defend the Constitution of the United States and the American people."

Walking on, I wondered if Gramps could hear me. I hoped he could. I imagined what he might say.

"Garvey, my grandson. You've rafted across the country. Might as well take a dip in the Chesapeake." "How about a shower at the Naval Academy?" "Not bad. Especially when the taxpayer picks up the bill." "You're just jealous." "You bet I am." "Well, I'm having dinner here, too." "Probably sleeping over in a dorm at the government's expense." "How'd you know?" "Figured. Of course, I can't blame you. Beats Motel 6." "I'll think of you, Gramps." "I know." "By the way, the research is coming along. Really moving." "Captain Patterson has been a big help, Garvey?" "You know he has." "Wait until he tells you what his dad did."

"You know?" "I've dipped my toe into the naval history." "You could have shared. Kept me from flying across the country." "Feeling sorry for yourself, Garvey?" "Probably." "Look at the brighter side. You escaped from the dungeon. You got your head out of books, reports, dust, and dusty old manuscripts. You flew across the country to meet the Captain and deal with living history. So enjoy yourself."

Even from the "afterworld," or wherever Gramps was residing, he was still controlling and manipulating me—pushing me one way or another. Of course, in this situation, he was right on. I liked being at the Naval Academy.

"Any hints before the Captain comes back?" "Fix your bunk, polish your shoes, and give him a snappy salute." "Thanks." "You're welcome."

As promised, Captain Patterson met me on the third floor.

"Old Army buddy, believe it or not. Visiting. Each year we bet on the Army-Navy Game by phone. Like taking money from a baby as long as the midshipmen win. So let's get back to the subject at hand." "Fine with me." "My father, as you will recall, was working for the Navy's Planning and Control Division, which was established in late 1942 to assist the Navy in dealing with the technological and social changes the war brought about. Within the Division, another entity was created—a sub-division known as the Special Programs Unit (SPU). My father was transferred to it.

"One of its purposes was to take the initiative in planning and coordinating new policies concerning Negroes, who would now be inducted into the general services. This was mainly in regard to three things: enlistment, training, and placement. Naturally, someone was needed to run SPU. It wasn't my dad.

"It was Christopher Smith Sargent, the proverbial non-entity, who probably shouldn't have been in the Navy and almost wasn't. His eyes were not 20/20. He had to wear glasses. This almost washed him out. The Navy granted him a waiver. However, he was never permitted to go to sea. He became a Navy bureaucrat. He sat at a desk. This turned out to be a good thing.

"My dad would be his assistant.

"Sargent was something of an expert at finance and logistical supplies. He had a nice way with people, especially politicians and higher Navy brass. He had a very flexible mind and a keen sense of when to compromise. He would spend 38 months in the SPU, during which time he proved to be the catalyst who solved the Navy's 'Negro problem' within the constraints of the day.

"He was by training a lawyer. On the basis of his belief in the need for innate fairness in the country's society, he was a crusader. Prior to entering the Navy, he had clerked for Supreme Court Justice Benjamin N. Cardozo, a liberal member of the Court. For him, it was a matter of simple elementary justice that all Americans should have equal opportunities.

"Sargent understood two realities: First, segregation in the Navy could not be ended immediately, in one fell swoop. Just not possible... Second, what was needed were a few experiments to determine what Negroes could do in the Navy, and by such demonstrations prove to critics that currently held views were inaccurate. Today, we might call this an incremental approach based on empirical results. Obviously, Sargent was trying to avoid being too precipitous where race was concerned."

"Captain Patterson, he wanted to conduct a controlled experiment?" "In a nutshell, yes." "What kind of experiment?"

"Garvey, I'm sure you've guessed."

I had. Sometimes 2 plus 2 actually equals 4. The President + Eleanor + the Navy's manpower needs + the Negro vote = an unusual experiment similar to what was happening in the Army with the Black paratroopers.

"Two ships, Garvey, would be commissioned with the purpose of eventually having an all-Black crew trained for each of them. One would be a destroyer-escort (the USS Mason); the other would be a submarine chaser (PC 1264). It was understood each ship would escort convoys, one across the Atlantic, the other ship would do escort duty along the eastern seaboard of the United States.

"There was logic to this plan. By escorting other ships, this meant that in a timely fashion they would always return to American ports. This was an exceedingly important point. Each ship had to be inspected before and after each assignment. The crew had to be questioned. Logbooks had to be reviewed. The white training officers and the Chiefs aboard ship had to attest to the progress of the Black seamen. The abilities of each sailor would be scrutinized.

"It was the SPU's responsibility to detail the enlisted Black sailors for training on land in every rating (skills) needed aboard a seagoing ship. In other words, sea training would begin on land. Experienced petty officers had to be found who would go to sea with the enlistees, who only had theoretical classroom experience. The white officers would leave the ship only when each sailor had competency at his rating at sea.

"The two-ship experiment would determine by actual experience the skills of Black sailors. By actual experience, the long-held opinions of the Navy would be tested against real-time realities... Only in this way could the true capabilities of the Black sailor be determined.

"By necessity, each ship would initially be segregated with only a few whites aboard. Mainly, as understood, the officers... Eventually, if all officers were replaced, including the captain, the ship would be totally Black. This would almost happen on the Mason. It did happen on the PC 1264.

"A lot was riding on the experiment. At its inception, no one really knew how it would turn out. Nothing like this had ever been done. I'm proud to say my father was part of the planning and implementation of the effort." "The President was aware of this?" "As was Mrs. Roosevelt."

"The first Black sailors would be the 'guinea pigs?'" "A lot would be riding on their shoulders, Garvey." "That's quite a story, Captain." "Isn't it? Permit me to say one more thing on behalf of Sargent." "Please." "He received the Legion of Merit for his actions during WWII. This award came for exceptional meritorious conduct in the performance of outstanding services to the Government of the United States as Assistant in the Office of the Director of Planning and Control and as Assistant Director of the Planning and Control Bureau of Naval Personnel from October 1942 to August 1945. I'm quite proud of what he did for the Navy and for Blacks in the Navy." "As rightfully you should be."

I enjoyed a first-class meal with a host of future naval officers later that day. Captain Patterson was my constant companion, sharing with me bits of Academy history, including curious pranks and bewildering traditions. I was a ready recipient of his endless narrative. As I was about to turn in for the evening, I thought of Gramps. How he would have enjoyed this day. And how much I missed him.

"Tomorrow, the archives, Gramps." "Find out about their training, Garvey." "And the men, too," I added. "And the men too."

CHAPTER 12

THE GREAT LAKES NAVAL STATION

THE NEXT DAY

The early morning flight from Baltimore to Chicago was uneventful, if one discounts the non-stop jabber of the heavyset, middle-aged man seated next to me. Dressed in an awful purple sport coat, he badgered my ear with a continuous, forgettable monologue. It wasn't that I was uninterested or insensitive to my fellow traveler—I just wanted a quiet flight, oblivious to the world's turmoil and the travails of daily life. But no such luck.

"The White Sox are as bad as ever," he lamented. "No hitting. No pitching. No fielding. Ownership stinks. Manager is out to lunch."

You buy your flight ticket and get a reserved seat, but who sits next to you is up to the gods. As the old adage goes, you can't choose the family you're born into. The same holds true for the stranger occupying the seat next to you.

Now I ask you—what could I say? I tried to be sympathetic. It wasn't easy.

"Sounds like you've covered the distresses of our Seattle team," I offered. "The shortstop is so bad, as the old joke goes, he couldn't catch a cold. And the other players? They never saw a high-and-away pitch they didn't like, adding K's to the opposing pitcher's stats. As for the manager? He's great at filling out the lineup card. After that…"

I was really pouring it on, hoping my baseball lament might quiet my fellow passenger. I was wrong.

"The Cubs!" he exploded. "It's our curse to live with a hex on the team. I don't know who did it, but we've got the black spot. Maybe some Egyptian mummy hates Chicago. Hell, the North Koreans might have done it."

"But you won the World Series in 2016!" I reminded him.

"Yeah, but nothing since."

"One trophy would be neat. Ask folks in Seattle."

"2016… That was a tease."

I was having trouble keeping up with my baseball buddy. Logic seemed to be the victim of his tirade. He had no empathy for my home city's struggles. I decided to throw a curveball of my own.

"Aliens have been known to do this sort of thing," I ventured.

"Aliens? Are you kidding me?"

"Not in the least. We know intelligent life exists beyond this flight." (And, I thought, probably beyond the seat adjacent to me.) "We're probably being watched even as we speak."

"Friend, I think you've had too much to drink. Christ, it isn't even 9:00 a.m. You need to rest."

With that, my erstwhile companion turned to his newspaper, leaving me to ponder intergalactic possibilities.

O'Hare Airport swallowed up the small, two-engine Mazda 800 commuter plane with one big gulp of the "windy city." Not long after, the bustling terminal spat me out into a questionable upgraded rental—a turbocharged, two-cylinder VW Prowler that promised 72 mpg. Since I was traveling less than 50 miles, it seemed like a good bet, assuming I didn't take a wrong turn.

I didn't.

As I drove to the Great Lakes Naval Training Center, located in what some call North Chicago in Lake County, I refreshed my memory about why I was here in Abe's good old state.

The men of the USS Mason and the PC-1264 were trained here, at the Navy's largest training base in the country. Curiously, the training center was located a thousand miles from either the Pacific or the Atlantic, which seemed absurd at first—placing a naval facility in the heart of the country, Great Lakes notwithstanding. Yet, as with many things, there was a rational explanation, especially when business, patriotism, and military needs aligned perfectly.

The base was opened in 1911 on land donated by the Merchants Club of Chicago. These businessmen, imbued with chest-thumping nationalism after the Spanish-American War, were budding imperialists delighted by the territorial gains of the conflict—Cuba, Puerto Rico,

Guam, and the Philippines. Their donation was both a show of respect for the Navy, which had wrought an empire, and a calculated investment. A vast naval training center, they reasoned, would be good for business.

The Merchants Club promoted Chicago as the ideal location for the envisioned training center, citing:

Geography: Chicago's proximity to the Great Lakes provided an ideal inland training site, with waters resembling inland seas.

Transportation: As the nation's railroad hub, Chicago offered an efficient, cost-effective means of transporting recruits and supplies.

Population: Chicago's diverse and sprawling population was a treasure trove of potential recruits.

Entertainment: The city promised ample distractions for sailors on liberty, from museums and markets to upscale restaurants—and, of course, seedier locales catering to every human indulgence. Whether Chicago's two baseball teams fell under "entertainment" remains debatable.

Given all these factors, the Navy accepted the Merchants Club's offer, and the Great Lakes Naval Station was born—a product of enterprising men and military necessity.

President Teddy Roosevelt had initially supported the idea in 1905. The base revolutionized naval training. Before its establishment, recruits were trained directly aboard ships, learning on the job while underway. This method was effective during peacetime or limited conflicts but was impractical for training thousands of men during larger wars. World War I highlighted the urgent need for centralized training facilities that could prepare recruits en masse.

Great Lakes provided the solution. The sprawling base covered over 1,600 acres, with more than 1,153 facilities and 39 major buildings, many designed by renowned architect Jarvis Hunt. Among these, Building

#1—also known as the "clock tower building"—stood out as Hunt's masterpiece. Built in 1911 from red bricks, the three-story structure featured a clock tower rising 300 feet above the ground, becoming a symbol of the base and its enduring legacy.

THE CLOCK TOWER

Given the size of the base and the number of trainees, it wasn't surprising that the Navy maintained its own fire and police departments and managed its own public works, including 50 miles of roads. The base functioned as a small, self-contained town.

The Great Lakes Training Center proved invaluable, particularly during World War II. By the end of the conflict, the base could accommodate 75,000 recruits at a time. During the war, more than one million men—over one-third of the Navy's total personnel—passed through the base, including Black seamen.

Camp Robert Smalls operated as a base-within-a-base for Black recruits, effectively keeping them segregated from white trainees. Railroad tracks running through the Great Lakes Training Center served as the boundary line, physically and symbolically separating the two groups. According to the Navy, this arrangement was necessary to train both groups on the same base while adhering to segregation policies. For Black recruits, this segregation was the price of combat training. However, from the perspective of the NAACP, the facility represented progress—a significant step forward as the first dedicated training center for Black sailors, staffed by competent white officers.

Despite the improved training opportunities, existing Naval policy barred Black sailors from combat roles, regardless of their preparation. Something more was needed to transform the Navy's perspective—and that change was already in motion.

After entering the facility, parking, and taking pictures of the iconic "clock tower," I headed to the base library. Thanks to Professor Richmond, whose network seemed boundless, I gained access to the archives related to "the experiment." I had planned to spend three days immersed in the past, but history had other plans for me. Two emotionally charged weeks would pass before I left.

For the first time, I came face-to-face with the Black sailors of the USS Mason and the PC-1264, who had trained at this base. It was an experience I would never forget.

CHAPTER 13

THE MEN

LORENZO DUFAU – USS MASON

Lorenzo DuFau lived in New Orleans when the war began. He was married with one child, a little boy. Because of his family responsibilities, he was classified 3-A, meaning he wouldn't be drafted. Yet, DuFau was determined to join the fight. A thoughtful and conscientious man, he had learned about the atrocities happening to Jews in Europe and felt a moral obligation to act. For him, volunteering was a twofold mission: to contribute to the fight against injustice abroad and to challenge the oppressive grip of Jim Crow laws that shaped life for his family at home.

Lorenzo DuFau learned from local Black newspapers that the Navy planned to open ratings to Black sailors, offering opportunities beyond the usual mess attendant roles. DuFau was familiar with that job—he made $90 a month as a mess attendant for nurses in a hospital, a good income for a Black man at the time, especially with civil service protection. But kitchen work in the Navy wasn't what he wanted.

DuFau longed for more. He was tired of Jim Crow laws, like the wooden screen on New Orleans trolleys labeled "Colored Patrons," a barrier moved back and forth to segregate passengers. When he enlisted, he resolved to challenge such systemic racism.

After induction, DuFau traveled to the Great Lakes Training Center with two other recruits by train. A Navy personnel officer in New Orleans made their travel arrangements, securing a roomette and meals in the dining car—a rare privilege for Black men in the Deep South. For the first time, they dined in a first-class dining car. Though many white passengers stared, there were no incidents—just silent discomfort.

However, being in the Navy didn't exempt recruits from racism. Upon arriving at the base late at night, no dinner was available. The next morning, the recruits enjoyed a hearty breakfast of baked beans, corned beef, cornbread, and coffee. For them, Uncle Sam's hospitality seemed promising.

"Gramps, do you believe this racial stuff?"

"As American as apple pie."

"Meaning?"

"Our country wasn't perfect then. Still isn't."

"It was so wrong."

"What do you want, Garvey—a perfect world?"

"That would be nice."

"Don't hold your breath."

"What are you saying, Gramps?"

"Utopia isn't around the corner."

"So?"

"Push for progress. One step at a time. Bigger steps, if possible, like Mr. Lincoln's Thirteenth Amendment."

"You're being cynical."

"I'm a realist. And by the way, how did you like DuFau's coffee story?"

How did Gramps know about that? I had just discovered the coffee story that morning, written in longhand by someone who interviewed DuFau years ago. The story was enough to make you angry—or at least want to hit something.

DuFau's coffee story took place during his nine-day leave after initial training at Great Lakes. On his way home to New Orleans and back, he encountered the harsh reality of segregation. In Atlanta, Georgia, during his return trip, he stopped at a station lunch counter in his Navy uniform to order coffee. Despite two urns brimming with coffee, the attendant refused him service. The stark contradiction struck him: he was ready to defend America, but America wouldn't serve him a simple cup of coffee.

DuFau was furious but refused to let such experiences discourage him. He vowed to persevere and not allow the Navy to treat him as a second-class citizen. The coffee incident became a symbol of the Jim Crow system he was determined to rise above.

Winfrey Roberts – USS Mason

Winfrey Roberts hailed from North Carolina and came from what he called a "distinguished family." His grandfather had been postmaster in Rich Square during Reconstruction, and his brother was once the registrar of deeds. Seeking freedom from Jim Crow laws and better opportunities, the family eventually moved to Orange, New Jersey.

Roberts left high school four months before graduation, promising his father he'd finish through night school. At 17, he moved to Washington, D.C., where he passed a civil service exam and landed a job with the War Department. After Pearl Harbor, he volunteered for the Coast Guard but was rejected. Soon after, he was drafted into the Navy.

In February 1943, Roberts traveled to the Great Lakes Naval Station with four other Black recruits. The Navy had reserved a club car for them, and though they encountered stares and whispers, there were no incidents. Arriving in a bitterly cold Chicago, Roberts found Camp Smalls to be a segregated world—something he was used to after his time in the nation's capital, where he couldn't even buy a hot dog at a soda fountain.

Determined to help defeat the Axis Powers and create change for his people, Roberts embraced the challenge, ready for the long haul.

Benjamin Garrison – USS Mason

Benjamin Garrison grew up in Columbia, South Carolina, and worked for the federal government when the war began. He enlisted in the Navy with dreams of "seeing the world," inspired by promises of fair treatment under a new rating system.

Boot camp at Great Lakes was transformative. It transitioned civilians into sailors, taught teamwork, and developed leadership skills. Garrison aimed for a higher rating, determined to rise above the lowest rank of seaman. He attended quartermaster school, where he learned navigation, steering, and weather forecasting. The ultimate goal was to become a chief petty officer, one of the Navy's elite.

But for Black sailors, advanced training didn't guarantee fair assignments. While white graduates were sent to warships, Black sailors were often relegated to shore facilities, creating tensions. White sailors resented that Black sailors weren't sent to combat, while Black sailors chafed at being excluded.

The segregation and prejudice extended beyond the base. In New Jersey, Black sailors assigned to Cape May Air Base were refused service at a local café, despite having government meal tickets. When the manager called the Shore Patrol, they diffused the situation by transporting the sailors to the base for food. A near riot was averted. At a Wildwood movie theater, Black sailors defied segregation by sitting in the center section. Supported by white sailors, the theater manager reluctantly allowed integrated seating.

Such incidents reflected the paradox Black sailors faced: they were fighting for freedom abroad while enduring discrimination at home.

Researching the Past

Research often uncovers unexpected treasures, like a photograph of Company 833 on the parade grounds in 1943. The long, clean lines of men bristled with questions: How did they end up at Great Lakes? Did they know they were part of a social experiment? What were their dreams after the war?

Other photos, like one of the Camp Robert Smalls drama group rehearsing in 1943, showed a different side of military life—stories of resilience, talent, and determination, beyond just the arts of war.

Each face in these photos carried a story, and those stories came together on the USS Mason and the PC-1264. Boot camp taught more than discipline and tactics; it forged bonds, fostered ambition, and laid the foundation for the men to challenge the status quo—both within the Navy and beyond.

THE DRAMA GROUP

Taken in 1943, another photo showed Black recruits receiving machine shop instruction. The professionalism of the white instructor and the complete attention of the Black seamen were vividly captured by the camera. In another photo, a recruit was shown receiving radio training.

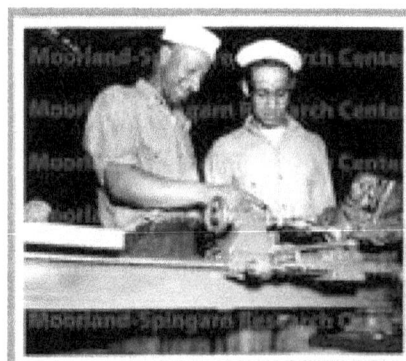

TRAINING

Graduation was a time of happiness and accomplishment at Camp Smalls, as one photo vividly captured. The graduates had completed their specialty training (rating) and stood erect and proud. If permitted to go to sea, the Navy was confident they could do the job. In theory, they had been thoroughly trained for duty. What was needed now was actual on-ship experience. Yet, a disquieting question loomed over the graduation ceremony: Would the graduates be given the opportunity to serve their country in combat roles?

PROUD GRADUATES

Celebrities often attended the graduation ceremonies, as evidenced by a scattering of photos. One shows Mrs. Joe Louis at a graduation parade. Here, I have a confession: I had never heard of her husband, nor did I understand why he was a celebrity. A quick check of my Apple X14 Smart Wrist Watch provided me with the essential information.

Joe Louis was the greatest heavyweight prizefighter according to Ring Magazine. He held the championship for twelve years, from 1937 to 1949, winning 72 out of 75 fights, with 57 knockouts. He was the first Black fighter to achieve nationwide status as a cultural hero—not only to Black Americans but also to the larger society.

JOE LEWIS

Two of Joe Louis's greatest fights were against the same man: Max Schmeling, the German national champion. Max won their first fight in 1936—a major upset. The rematch took place three years later at Yankee Stadium on June 22, 1938. Over 70,000 people attended, while millions more listened on their radios.

What made the fight so significant was the political context. Though Max was not a member of the Nazi Party, he represented Germany and, by extension, the Nazi regime that preached "Aryan superiority"—a view disturbingly reminiscent of the Black Codes and Jim Crow laws. In stark and ugly terms, Hitler's followers believed that no Black man could defeat a white man, especially Max.

The fight, scheduled for 15 rounds, lasted just 2 minutes and 4 seconds into the first round. Louis pummeled Schmeling, knocking him down three times before the fight was stopped. Known as the "Brown Bomber," Louis emerged victorious. Germany despaired. America cheered. Bigots wept.

LOUIS VICTORIOUS

Having Mrs. Joe Louis attend the graduation at Camp Robert Smalls was a significant honor.

Photo # 80-G-294888 Mrs. Joe Louis at graduation parade, Great Lakes, 1943

MRS. LOUIS VISITS

The celebrities in a second photo were ones I did recognize. Who wouldn't? President Franklin D. Roosevelt and his wife, Eleanor, visited

Camp Robert Smalls in 1943. They spent considerable time reviewing the facility and speaking with officers and men alike. The President liked to ask about the food, while Eleanor was more interested in the training. Keeping things close to the vest, the President was already considering the "great experiment." Together, they were ensuring that "Mrs. Roosevelt's folly" was giving Black sailors every opportunity to succeed. Quite a team...

THE FIRST FAMILY

Research is a fickle creature—more like a wild horse sometimes, taking you in directions you hadn't considered. And that's what happened to me.

I came across a name: Doris Miller, who had received the Navy Cross Citation while serving as a mess attendant on the USS West Virginia, a powerful battleship with sixteen-inch guns. Immediately, I asked myself how a woman could earn this medal, second only to the Congressional Medal of Honor.

And that's when I learned about "Dorie," as Doris Miller was known to his shipmates.

He had been on the West Virginia when the Japanese attacked early Sunday morning, December 7, 1941. Due to his physical prowess, he was assigned to carry wounded sailors below deck to safer places. This included carrying the mortally wounded captain of the ship, who was dying on the bridge. After that, he manned a .50 caliber Browning anti-aircraft machine gun until he ran out of ammunition and was ordered to abandon ship. It appears he shot down one plane, even though he had never fired such a weapon before the attack. He was awarded the Navy Cross for his actions.

The West Virginia's crew numbered 1,541; 130 were killed that fateful day, and 52 were wounded. Two armor-piercing bombs eventually sank the ship in Pearl Harbor's shallow waters.

Dorie Miller's Navy Cross Citation read:

"For distinguished devotion to duty, extraordinary courage, and disregard for his own personal safety during the attack on the Fleet in Pearl Harbor, Territory of Hawaii, by Japanese forces on December 7, 1941. While at the side of his captain on the bridge, Miller, despite enemy strafing and bombing and in the face of serious fire, assisted in moving his captain, who had been mortally wounded, to a place of greater safety, and later manned and operated a machine gun directed at enemy Japanese attacking aircraft until ordered to leave the bridge."

Dorie Miller, as it turns out, became the first Black hero of World War II. He became an inspiration to other Black seamen and, especially, for his campaign for equal recognition and opportunity for all persons in the armed forces.

Miller was presented the Navy Cross by Fleet Admiral Chester W. Nimitz, the Commander in Chief of the Pacific Fleet, on board the aircraft carrier USS Enterprise. In presenting the medal, Nimitz said on May 22, 1942:

"This marks the first time in this conflict that such high tribute has been made in the Pacific Fleet to a member of his race, and I'm confident the future will see others similarly honored for brave acts."

THE FIRST HERO

I thought about the Admiral's remark: "Similarly honored... Member of his race... High tribute..."

I wondered, would the "Navy's experiment" finally give the Black sailors training at the Great Lakes Naval Base the opportunity Nimitz had cited?

But before that, they would need ships to defend.

Somewhere over the distant horizon, the plans for two ships were being drawn—two ships that would change history.

CHAPTER 14

YOU GOTTA HAVE LOVE

THREE WEEKS LATER – SEATTLE

It was raining today. The forecast promised rain tomorrow, and into next week and beyond. This was Seattle.

The rain didn't bother me. Sheltered in the UW Library, deeply buried in the literary catacombs of the immense building, I heard no pelting of rainwater, driven almost horizontally by gusting winds, against the crimson-colored brick construction dating back to an earlier century. Back from my successful trip to the Naval Academy, I was once again completely absorbed in my work. I had a safe refuge in my self-imposed subterranean lair.

Unless the whole place sprung an unexpected Grand Coulee Dam leak, I was high and dry in my bookish, earthy redoubt.

Before me lay three stacks of research notes and primary documents, which needed review to write a sensible narrative that would tease out another aspect of the USS Mason and PC 1264 story. Some of the documents came from the shipbuilders—Bethlehem Steel Company (Boston) and Consolidated Shipbuilding Co. (New York City). Other material had been made available through the Pentagon's archives. Lastly, family members of former seamen on the two ships had graciously provided letters and diaries.

Looking at the research stacks, I figured I had enough material to outlast the storm above Puget Sound and anything else Canada's fickle weather might throw at my beloved town. That the storm might wash out a few Mariners baseball games never occurred to me. Seen from one perspective, that might be considered a good thing, given their standing in the American League's West Division. I didn't verbalize that thought.

What I hadn't figured on was the reappearance of the co-ed who had indirectly, if not quite modestly, invited me to a dance.

She entered my research world, spied me, and walked briskly in my direction, her long black hair today falling to her shoulders, her dark eyes bright and feisty, as was her walk. She wore tightly hugging Levi pants and a heavy UW jacket still coated with moisture from the day's rain. A full backpack bounced against her shoulders, adorned with a patch showing Mickey Mouse in a sailor's outfit. An old rain hat was partially squeezed into it. My research penchant for noticing details was proving useful.

Reaching my bunker, she said, "You've returned."

What could I say? I tried to be cool. "The prodigal researcher cometh."

"Very catchy."

"Spur of the moment stab at seeming literate."

I felt so dumb. Why was I acting this way? Usually, I didn't stab at anything unless I was lost in a steakhouse. Why was this beautiful co-ed making me feel so darn uneasy? She hadn't the first time we met. Or had she?

"No need to stab, Professor Langston. I've checked you out."

"Just a run-of-the-mill grad student."

"Not for long, from what I've heard."

I had to admit it. "Professor Langston" sounded quite nice. But who was spouting such rumors? I decided not to ask.

"Perhaps someday…"

"You're also getting a reputation as a cool teacher. Imagine, an entire seminar discussing just one day."

"Actually, we do have a prologue and an epilogue, not just May 8, 1945."

"Your students like you."

Again, what could I say? What teacher doesn't want to be liked? Beats being beaten over the head with a broken banjo.

"Some of your female students think you're kind of cute."

That did it. What's a guy supposed to do? I was flattered. I was also curious. Okay, the truth was, my ego was in full massage mode.

"You have spies in my class?"

"Informants on the volleyball team."

"You play?"

"Team manager."

For some reason, I needed to change the subject…

"Did you go to the Beatles' Dance?"

"Danced all night."

THE BEATLES

Jealousy was something that happened to others. At least, until that moment… Suddenly, I could see hordes of robust males dancing with my fantasy date. It was a terrible image assailing me. I tried desperately to hide my feelings.

"Perhaps… if there's another dance…"

"Tomorrow."

"You're going?"

"Of course."

"Would you…"

"I live just off campus at…"

And that's how I got my first date as a grad student. And with Evelyn, something much more than a mirage…

"I don't remember your name. Eve? Elaine? Elizabeth?" I asked, knowing full well it wasn't.

"Evelyn. And you're Garvey."

Garvey and Evelyn… It sounded kind of nice. The more I said it, the nicer it sounded.

"Tell me about your thesis, Garvey."

So I did. It took a few minutes. Okay, more like an hour. I'll admit it. I stretched things out.

"That's quite an enterprise."

"Occupies most of my time."

"Unless you're going to a dance."

An exception I was now surprisingly desirous of making. "I'd like that," I said quietly.

With that, Evelyn turned to her studies, a faint smile cloaking her face, and I returned to my ships, my heart beating a little faster than usual. Later she departed, simply saying as she did, "I'll expect you at eight." And with that, she left.

And for the longest moment, I was desolate.

"Gramps, what's happening?"

"Topic sentence here?"

"Evelyn."

"Oldest story in the world."

"But new to me."

"In a word, you entered the 'wow' moment."

"Meaning?"

"Your heart is beating faster?"

"Yes."

"You're feeling a tingling sensation?"

"Yes."

"You feel like something is missing in your life?"

"Yes."

"That's the 'wow' moment."

"Does that mean?"

"Yes, Garvey, Cupid has struck."

"What do I do?"

"Go to the dance."

It took an extra effort to refocus on my research.

CHAPTER 15

TRADITIONS

The U.S. Navy has many traditions—what some might call rituals or ingrained customs. For a ship about to enter the fleet, the milestone is known as commissioning, a public ceremony that marks the moment when the officers and crew, having been tested for competency, are officially installed. It is also the final step in a triad of activities: laying the ship's keel, launching and christening the ship, and, finally, commissioning.

It is the moment when the local Naval District Commandant transfers the ship to the Captain by reading a commissioning directive. The Captain then assumes command, with responsibility for maintaining the ship—a man-of-war—both in peace and during wartime.

A commissioned ship enters active Navy service, a ritual that dates back to 1785, when the Alfred, the first ship of the Continental Navy, was commissioned in Philadelphia.

THE ALFRED

The new crew stands at attention during commissioning. The national anthem is played, and a commissioning pennant is raised on the mast.

The pennant is typically a long streamer in a version of America's national colors—usually blue at the hoist, adorned with seven white stars and two longitudinal stripes of red and white. It is flown proudly at all times, symbolizing the ship's protection, especially in battle. The ceremony concludes with the Captain setting the first watch.

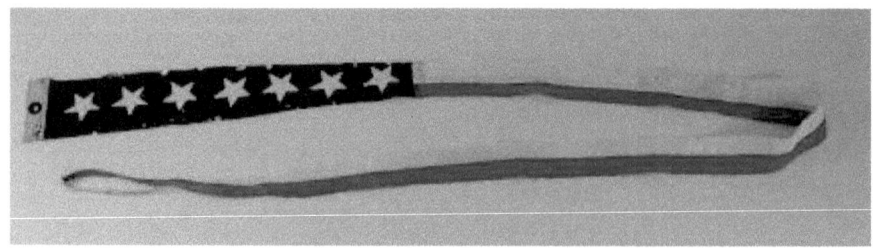

THE LONG STREAMER

For the USS *Mason* (DE-529), the crucial date was March 20, 1944. One month later, the PC 1264 joined the fleet on April 25, 1944.

COMPARISON CHART

USS MASON (DE-529)	FACTOR	PC 1264
March 20, 1944	Date Commissioned	April 25, 1944
Bethlehem Steel	Builder	Consolidated
Boston	Location	New York City
239 feet	Length	173 feet
35 feet	Beam	23 feet
21 knots	Speed	19 knots
156 crew members	Crew Size	65 in crew
Depth charges	Major Weapon	Depth charges

THE USS MASON

The *Mason* was a new type of ship: a destroyer escort. It was smaller than a destroyer but larger than a coastal patrol craft, and at $5,000,000, it was relatively inexpensive to build. By the war's end, 565 destroyer escorts would be built, many by Bethlehem Steel's shipyard in Quincy, Massachusetts, where 66 were constructed. Four would not survive the war.

USS MASON DE 529

These ships, the destroyer escorts (DE), were sometimes referred to as the "poor man's destroyer." Others called them ships of the "Donald Duck Navy," though more graciously, they were often called "small boys." Their mission was three-fold: First, to protect convoys, especially in the North Atlantic. Second, to find and destroy German U-boats, which posed a serious threat. The undersea menace sank over 1,100 ships, resulting in the loss of over 40,000 sailors during the war. Third, if necessary, the destroyer escort was considered expendable. That is, if ordered, it would place itself between a troop ship and an incoming torpedo. As one crewmember on the Mason, Benjamin Garrison, recalled:

"We knew that if a submarine targeted a torpedo at, say, a troop carrier, the Escort Commander could tell a destroyer escort to get between that ship and the torpedo. We had fewer men, we were a small ship, and it was important that the larger ship survive."

Depth charges were the primary weapon aboard the Mason. These were 50-gallon drums containing 600 pounds of high explosives, which were dropped or projected off the destroyer escorts. Submariners of every navy feared them.

DEPTH CHARGE

Before a submarine could be destroyed, it had to first be located. Both the Mason and the PC 1264 were equipped with sophisticated tracking systems, including the latest radar, sonar, and radio technology. Sound waves were used to detect the metal "fish" lurking in the depths.

These sound waves were sent out and the returning echoes analyzed. Was it a whale? A school of fish? A U-boat? These electronic "ears" made it increasingly difficult for submarines to sneak into a convoy and take an uncontested shot.

PC 1264

The PCs, or "patrol crafts," were essentially sub-chasers, especially along the eastern seaboard of the United States. Their primary role was to escort and protect convoys, particularly those transporting oil tankers from the Gulf of Mexico. Like the destroyer escorts, the PCs were also considered expendable. A total of 369 were produced during the war. Unfortunately, except for the relic I discovered in the graveyard, no PC was preserved after the war, with one notable exception: a sister ship in the Arthur Kill, which was largely forgotten and, at the time, undetected by me.

PC CLASS WARSHIP

Though over 50,000 young men served on the PCs, their exploits were largely forgotten. In the case of the PC 1264, some might argue it was "purposely forgotten." It became my obligation, I realized, to change all of that.

Due to their small size and relatively large crew for the ship's dimensions, everything aboard the PCs was more personal. Cramped quarters induced less formality, and the ship's constant motion—pitching and rolling—led to seasickness. Sailors aboard larger ships were often amazed at the tremendous battering a heavy sea could inflict on a PC.

One humorous story captures this well. The PC 486 was escorting an American submarine home from a war patrol through rough seas, with waves towering above most of the PC. At times, the submarine's officers couldn't even see the surface ship. On one occasion, as the two ships rose above the waves in unison, the sub's skipper signaled the PC, asking the captain if he would like a periscope. The reply came back, "Thanks, but we're below periscope depth." Such was the humor at sea.

Both the destroyer escort and patrol craft were built under the Emergency Shipbuilding Program following Pearl Harbor. Frank Knox, the Secretary of the Navy, emphasized the importance of this program early in the war. He acknowledged the obvious: the nation was at war, and there was no time for labor disputes. Ships—and more ships—were needed to confront the enemy on two fronts. From Knox's perspective, the Navy had to lead the nation.

Knox's call resonated with the civilian workforce. The prevailing sentiment in the shipyards was that everyone had a role to play. The harder the workers built ships, the faster the war would end. For those in the shipyards, PCs and destroyer escorts represented a crucial step in securing victory.

FRANK KNOX

When a ship is commissioned, every member of the crew at that moment is known as a "plank-owner." In other words, they are part of the original crew. Each shipmate was given a certificate to commemorate this honor. The certificate was ornate, often bordered with nautical illustrations in vivid colors. It resembled the work of a scribe copying a page from the Bible in a medieval monastery, honoring his God with reverence, obedience, and faith. Beautiful to read, beautiful to look at. But more than that, the certificate acknowledged each sailor's commitment to defending the United States of America—a pledge not taken lightly in the global slaughterhouse that was 1944.

The first crews of both ships would be plank-owners.

"Garvey, stifle the research for a moment."

"Gramps?"

"Yes, unless you've got another cranky old guy rummaging around in your noggin?"

"Just you, I'm afraid."

"I'll take that as a compliment. Now that we've got past that, how about our own plank-owner?"

"Your dad?"

"Your great-great grandfather, Sam. Time to put him in the footnotes, don't you think?"

"Samuel Langston, 1943 – Brooklyn Naval Yard – the USS Saufley (DD 465) is launched, and he's a member of the original crew. Stayed with the ship until late 1944 before a heart attack got to him. Not that the Japanese hadn't sought the pleasure. He received a Purple Heart for wounds received off the Philippines."

"Hit by a suicide plane, if I remember correctly."

"Kamikaze. Almost sank the destroyer. Now for some family trivia, Garvey... Two items. The DD 465 was the second most decorated destroyer in the war, receiving 16 battle stars. Bet you didn't know that."

"Safe bet. You won. The next item?"

"No one knows what happened to his plank-owner certificate. Just disappeared into history."

We left it there. Gramps slipped away, and I dug into my research notes.

The first Captain of the USS Mason was William M. Blackford. He was from Seattle, Washington.

CAPTAIN BLACKFORD

He wrote many letters during the war to his wife, including one about the ship's commissioning and the crew. His letters noted the following:

The ship was commissioned on March 23, 1944.

The ceremony took place during a blinding snowstorm.

The Mayor and the Governor made speeches.

Dr. and Mrs. Mason were present, as the ship was named after their son, Ensign Richard Mason.

The parents presented an oil portrait of their son, which was placed in the wardroom.

A colored society provided enough musical instruments to form a ship's band.

The crew is better than average and has a strong spirit.

Importantly: the Black sailors are no different from others if treated the same, which I do.

The members of the crew are anxious to make a name for our ship. I can't blame them.

They work harder than most recruits.

Typical of the crew was Merwin Peters, who later explained how he felt about being on the USS Mason:

"I went aboard that ship with stars in my eyes. This was a great opportunity. It fit in more with what I wanted to do, as opposed to maybe just sitting on some base somewhere having a sedentary job. It was an opportunity for travel, for adventure — all of the usual things that an eighteen-year-old has in mind."

As for the crew and officers, and "Eleanor's Folly"... Seaman Charles W. Divers, who shared his feelings after the war, said his experience aboard the Mason was bittersweet:

"I think the powers that be that opposed integration had programmed us to fail. The USS Mason was not expected to succeed. But when we started proving them wrong and succeeding, rather than eat crow, they downplayed all our accomplishments and virtues."

The Atlanta Daily News, a Negro newspaper, covered the commissioning of the Mason with a banner headline — "First Race-Manned War Ship in Service." The coverage was thorough, stating:

"With a cold bitter wind accompanying a steady snowfall on this first day of spring, the first U.S. Naval vessel with a predominantly Negro crew, the Destroyer Escort USS Mason, was placed in full commission Monday at Boston Navy Yard."

The article continued:

"The crew presently consists of 160 Negroes and 44 whites. It is anticipated that as soon as Negro personnel can be trained and qualified, they will replace the white ratings in their specialized billets, so that the entire crew eventually will be Negroes..."

It further noted:

"There was a moistness in the eyes of some of the colored workers who, with their white comrades, braved the bitter cold to witness the ceremony. They sensed that not only was this something they had helped fashion with their own hands and skill to be manned by their own boys, but that this was their opportunity to show the world they were just as capable under a welder's hood as machine-gunning an enemy plane and just as efficient at turning lathe as running down an enemy submarine."

Lorenzo A. Du Fau provided perspective on the "experiment" long after the war was over:

"You had these people, observers, come aboard; they were personnel officers. But we knew they were there to see how we'd do. And we were fully aware that we would be under the microscope, realizing the load that was on us. Looking back, I'm glad I didn't know as much then as I know now, because I probably would have been shaken up a bit to know what weight we had to carry."

Du Fau also said:

"… It was a puzzle to me why we had to be studied like something in a laboratory. We were human beings, blood running in our veins, loyal American citizens doing everything that was required. But when it came to working in the service, all of a sudden we were only qualified to serve meals or do just menial stuff. The weight of proving our ability was on us, opening the door for those who would come behind. It was really a double front we were up against."

COLD AND PROUD

What was said about the Mason was generally true of the PC 1264. Numerous invitations were mailed to families, friends, and naval officials, as well as to the Negro press. The Navy was encouraging publicity — radio, movies… Television, if it had existed then, would have received a major invite. Today's WWW (World Wide Web) would have been inundated with information. The social network would have been working overtime. But for its day, the Navy was temporarily lifting wartime censorship, even to the extent of letting reporters aboard the ship before the actual commissioning.

At exactly 11:30 a.m. on Tuesday, April 25, 1944, the ceremony took place at the Navy's Pier 42 on the lower west side of Manhattan. The Commanding Officer, Eric S. Purdon, who was a strong advocate for the PC class of ships, was well aware of the stakes involved with the PC 1264. He knew his ship was a guinea pig — to prove or disprove a hodgepodge of questionable beliefs about the Negro race that many Americans, as well as too many naval officers, held.

PURDON READING ORDERS

It was common currency that Blacks had serious physiological differences beyond the mere coloration of their skin. Some claimed his brain was smaller, therefore he could never be the intellectual equal of the white man. He was considered animalistic. Personal cleanliness was unimportant to him. These were outlandish views, but they were believed by many. Bunking the races together in the confined quarters of a ship would turn it into a pest house. Wasn't it true that a slave ship could be smelled from beyond the horizon? Conveniently, the inhuman living conditions aboard a slave ship were never mentioned — overcrowded ship holds, little food, no real latrines, and an absence of fresh air.

And added to all this was a final verdict: generally speaking, the Black sailor couldn't be depended on in battle.

These beliefs notwithstanding, the commissioning ceremony went off without a hitch. A Navy chaplain solicited the favor of a nondenominational God, and the band played a rousing rendition of The Stars and Stripes Forever. Then, with the passing of authority to the ship's master, the PC 1264 entered the fleet. As it did, the father of yeoman Paul G. Davis caught the Captain's ear, saying, "Take good care of our boy." Captain Purdon responded candidly, "I'm relying on him to take care of me."

It should be noted in passing that neither captain — Blackford nor Purdon — was aware that this was one military assignment they couldn't be ordered to take. Each commanding officer had to volunteer. Both were told that the duty would be a real headache. The Navy would be breathing down their necks, and the disciplinary problems might drive any officer mad. If you wanted command, you would have to sign a "proof of agreement." Neither captain was quite sure why the Navy had picked him for this special duty, but neither flinched from signing the "agreement."

CHAPTER 16

THE CAPTAINS

SEATTLE – A MONTH LATER

Let's be straight about this.

There is no public record suggesting that the two captains ever met in person. Nothing at all. Though chosen by the "anonymous bureaucratic powers" that played with names and ranks in Washington D.C., the choice of Eric S. Purdon and William M. Blackford to command the PC 1264 and the USS Mason respectively seems unrelated. The two men never trained together. They never served at the same naval base or aboard the same ship. Nor were they brought together, as one might have expected, to acquaint them with the "social experiment" concerning Blacks in the Navy. Had they passed each other in a long corridor of the Pentagon, they would not have recognized one another.

These thoughts were running through my mind.

I wondered: What might have happened if they had met, if not during the war, at least in its aftermath? What would they have said to each other? Were they not kindred spirits, each captaining a ship of social change?

There is a hint that Purdon was aware of the USS Mason. In his book Black Company (1972), Purdon mentions the DE-529, as well as the PC 1264, in his prologue, stating:

"These ships would demonstrate the practical parts of the experiment and, with the definitiveness of actual experience, prove or disprove the opinions many Americans held about the capabilities of a people."

Whether the two captains corresponded with each other prior to Purdon's book is unknown. Certainly, Purdon knew, with unbridled pride, that the experiment, though a full-fledged success, was, in one small way, a greater achievement for the smaller ship. The Mason was never able to transfer all the white petty officers, while the PC 1264 was able to do this and replace them with qualified Blacks. In that limited sense, the ultimate success of the experiment rested more on the patrol craft than the destroyer escort.

These are the unvarnished facts. Still, I wondered: what might they have discussed had the captains met?

I decided, as an intellectual challenge, to consider such an exchange, adhering to one restriction: everything written would be factual, strongly supported by at least three sources, even if dramatic prose was necessary at times. Whether Professor Richmond would indulge this form of thesis writing on my part, I was unsure.

ST. LOUIS - 1947

For the captains to meet, a location was needed — somewhere, I thought, where they would feel comfortable, and which was, of course, convenient. Thus, I conjured up the White Duck Restaurant in St. Louis. In my mind, it was known far and wide for its clam chowder, which was thick with creamy sauce, potatoes, and lots of clams, plus a secret seasoning that tempted emulation by others, generally without any real success. As for its other offerings, the White Duck provided a variety of savory fish fare sufficient to satisfy the needs of any mariner — salmon, cod, swordfish, bass... All freshly (or nearly freshly) caught. As for the wine list and the assortment of beers, the White Duck was — without question — well-supplied for its patrons.

A maritime motif gave the place a nautical feeling. On each wall, there were shelves with models of civilian and naval ships, each painstakingly constructed to precise ratios, and painted to exacting colors — expensive yachts, musty old bulk freighters, cavernous oil transports, and, of course, luxurious cruise liners. And then there were the warships — destroyers, cruisers, battleships, carriers, and submarines. Against each wall was the anchor from a famous ship, its rust removed and a healthy coat of paint added. There were symbols, too, of rank, especially the stars, shoulder boards, and sleeve stripes of a U.S. Navy captain, the senior-most commissioned officer rank below that of flag officer, such as an admiral.

The St. Louis was a perfect place for a meeting. And this is where I brought the captains together, in "Middle America." One captain had flown in from Seattle — that was Eric Purdon, who commanded the PT 1264. The other captain, William Blackford, flew in from New York City to represent the USS Mason.

And that's the way the two captains felt as they savored steaming hot, black coffee in a pugnacious white cup, oblong in its appearance. After a little small talk to break the ice — "Glad to meet you at last." — "How's your family?" — "Miss the old days?" — they got down to business.

"How did you find out, Eric, about your appointment to the 1264?"

"I was at home with my pregnant wife in Miami Beach. A Watch Officer called, telling me to 'proceed immediately' to Morris Heights, New York for the commissioning of the ship. I had twenty-four hours to get there, not the usual four days."

"No preliminaries?"

"None, William. Just haul stern and get there, which I did, even as our second child was born."

"Please call me Bill. What'd you think when you first saw the 1264?"

"It was a cold, snowy morning with gray skies — February 3, 1944, and boy, was she an ugly duck. Her superstructure was dappled with yellow zinc chromate. There were power cables festooned across her deck. They disappeared into the bowels of the ship, from which came a kaleidoscope of noise — the grinding of machinery, strange thumps, and the colorful cries of workmen. Bedlam... Hammers and torches below... Snowflakes above... The ship was a work in progress."

WIRES EVERYWHERE

"Tough first impression, Eric."

"Which I sought to expunge. I tried to imagine what she would eventually look like in time — slim and sleek, a long shaft of metal camouflaged with gray paint, gliding through dangerous waters at 20 knots or more, her flags and pennant stretched tightly by the wind. A lovely thought."

"Every captain loves his ship."

"Our mistress at sea, Bill."

"Why do you think you were chosen?"

"I just don't know."

"But you suspected…"

"I liked PCs. I had served on the PC 1252 for four months. Went to sea for seven days. I had studied sub-chasers — piloting, gunnery, diesel, and gasoline engines. Not bad for a guy born in the Philippines, who attended schools in England and Ireland, and earned a B.A. at Trinity College in Hartford."

"Not a social activist?"

"Not in the least. I think I was chosen simply because I was available. What about you, William?"

"I'm not sure. I was named the Mason's captain before it was decided to man her with a Black crew. Randomness… bureaucratic chance… karma… Beats me. The ship was being built even before I was picked."

"So you signed on, William?"

"As did you, Eric."

"Right. I was told I could turn down the assignment, which I declined to do. And like you, I was asked to sign a form stating for the record that I didn't mind serving with a 'colored crew.'"

"Tough to say no to the Navy."

"Doesn't lead to plush assignments, William."

"Eric, you were told the crew would be a 'pain in the ass?'"

"To say the least. So why did we sign on? What really motivated us? What was at the heart of our decision?"

"Try this one on for size... The challenge... And simple fairness... All guys should get a fair shake."

"That about sums it up, William. Of course, in your case, there may have been another reason for the Navy's choice."

"Such as?"

"Maybe it was because you were from Seattle? Lots of boating on Lake Washington, I hear."

"I did love our family yacht, the Sally Bruce. Learned my first seamanship on her. Attended the University of Washington. Earned a degree in chemistry. Moved on to the University of Virginia. Two classes away from my Ph.D. in chemistry when Uncle Sam put me on active duty... I was the XO on the USS Frigate Bird (AMC-20) and later the USS Pawtucket, an ocean-going tug. In '42 I took command of the USS Phoebe, a coastal minesweeper..."

"Off of Washington State, William?"

"Way off. How about the Aleutian Islands?"

"Then?"

"The Mason."

"Were you into civil rights?"

"Truth be told, I had hardly any Negro acquaintances before the Mason, at least not directly. You?"

"Ditto. But what did you mean by 'not directly?'"

CHAPTER 17 –

FAMILY SECRETS

Former Captain William M. Blackford smiled, took a long swig of coffee, then ordered another fill-up from an attentive waitress, along with the largest sugar-infested bear claw in town, which was quickly devoured. Watching this, Eric Purdon couldn't help but remark, "Those things can kill you."

"Well, they didn't call me 'Big Bill' for eating my vegetables. Just love to eat. Caught up to me after the war."

"Oh."

"Tried to enlist full-time in the Navy, but I failed the physical examination. I was forced to retire to civilian life."

"After all you went through!"

"Peacetime Navy could be selective. Want a bite?"

"No thanks. Now, what about...?"

"My great-grandmother. She was a noted abolitionist in Virginia. Mary Berkeley Minor Blackford..."

Mary Berkeley Minor Blackford
at 76

THE ABOLUTIONIST

"Never heard of her."

"Nor did the Navy, Eric. The Navy didn't know she was my ancestor."

"Quite a coincidence."

"She came from a slave-owning family in Fredericksburg. She was put off by the brutality of Virginia's slaveholding society. Along with her husband, William Blackford, she participated in the activities of the American Colonization Society, which sought to assist freed slaves in immigrating to Liberia. Together, they sponsored the passage of at least seven of their slaves to Liberia. Until Fort Sumter, she labored on behalf of gradual emancipation of slaves in Virginia. As war approached, she felt that secession was unpatriotic. This view alienated her from friends and family alike."

"Quite a lady."

"She even lobbied for the promotion of female education in Africa long before such views were in vogue."

"You were a crusader?"

"To beat Japan, yes. And Germany? Yes! To change society, no... I just went along with the Navy's experiment. Like you..."

"What a pair we make."

I stopped typing. The last words clung to the computer screen: "I just went along..."

I was exhausted. Every bone in my body felt fatigued. My fingers cramped, as if protesting what they knew must be written next.

Rather than continue, I wanted to leave my self-imposed dungeon. I wanted to go outside. Into the sun… Breathe fresh air…

I couldn't do that. There was no escape. Not yet, anyway… The captains weren't finished.

"The Mason was a good ship, William."
"As was the 1264, Eric."
"Sister ships."
"Bastard ships for some."

CHAPTER 19

UNWANTED

The words hung in the air. Unhappily, each captain knew in his heart what was referred to... And each had tried to defend his ship against these words...

"When did you first hear it, Bill?"

"Miami. We were docking the Mason. We threw the number one line over and yelled for a seaman to secure it to the pier. The seaman refused. He said he wasn't going to take no line off that ship, 'off no nigger ship.'"

"The word was out?"

"Wherever we went."

"You tied up?"

"Eventually. I got the seaman's name, rate, and service number. Passed the information up... Wanted the jerk dealt with."

"Was he?"

"Never knew."

"We ran into similar situations in Miami, Bill. The crew had liberty for almost a month. It was really an empty privilege. Jim Crow ordinances restricted where my men could go, even how late they could be on the streets. It was a misdemeanor for being on the street after the sun went down for 'colored' at Miami Beach."

"Gracious citizens."

"The crew could go to a snack bar at the shipyard. It was strictly segregated. Three sections — one for 'white,' one for 'colored,' and one for 'enlisted.' The woman serving the enlisted section refused to serve our guys. They were told to go to the section for their race."

"They got away with that?"

"Civilian establishment. Nothing the Navy could do, but object."

"Do you believe that?"

"Not really. It was wartime. The Navy brass could have flexed a few muscles."

"But an easier path was taken?"

"Yes. You mentioned situations…"

"George Pool, our executive officer, returned to the ship one night, alone. He showed his identification card to the civilian guards, who asked him, 'Are you from the nigger ship?' George gave a somewhat neutral answer to the two guards who had their hands on their .38 revolvers. 'I am attached to the USS PC 1254.' One of the guards, fat-bellied and big, got in George's face, saying, 'Let me tell you, you goddamn Yankee nigger-lover. See that building over there? We'll string you and your goddamn niggers to the top of it, if they give any more shit to our white women. Y'all tell 'em to keep away from our women.'"

"Your XO was cool."

"Just nodded, Bill. The last incident was weird. Another PC was docked near us with its white crew. The civilian guards were friendly to the white crew and antagonistic toward my guys. Then one day, the truculence stopped. No smiles… Certainly, no friendliness… But no trouble… It took me awhile to figure out what happened."

"The Navy jumped on the guards?"

"In a way, yes. White sailors from the other PC were drinking in a tavern near the shipyard entrance. They heard some 'good old boys' talking… Full of whiskey, the men were going down to the pier to shoot up 'that nigger ship.' The white sailors quietly left the tavern."

"To warn the 1264?"

"Better than that! They went back to their ship, broke into the small-arms locker and grabbed .45s and rifles. They then deployed themselves at the main gate after telling the surprised guards they were going to defend the 1264. The guards got the point. No invasion occurred. The guards acted better. Funny thing, though…"

"What?"

"The white sailors got away with this without telling their officers, including the Captain. Now, Bill, that's weird."

"Like nothing happened!"

"Exactly."

"Speaking of officers, Eric, I had a troublesome chief, a radio specialist. He was supposed to certify the competency of our radio guys, who had theoretical but not practical experience at sea. He just wouldn't help. Treated the men like they weren't there. Eventually, orders came through for all my chiefs to depart. They were ordered to the West Coast where they were needed for the invasion of Japan. As the belligerent chief was leaving, he turned and lashed out with his hatred of the Black sailors, saying, 'He didn't give a damn what happened to them.' He 'hoped some submarine would hit them and destroy every one of my black crew.'"

"Sweet Jesus."

"One of our guys yelled back, 'We love you, chief.' Then others joined in… 'We love you. We love you.'"

"Generally, the chiefs did a good job. Stuck to business… Didn't let their private thoughts interfere with the training. That guy was just a jerk."

"I agree. Navy couldn't do without the chiefs."

"You know, it's one thing to run into this stuff in our country. We have a long history — slavery, Jim Crow laws, discrimination and segregation… But to find it in London… That was a real surprise for the Mason's crew, Eric. And by our USO."

"What?"

"In London, they had separate USO (United Services Organization) services for Blacks. Our guys couldn't understand this. Weren't we allies of the British? Were we protecting the supplies coming to England? Weren't we sailors in the American Navy? Of course, we were, but that didn't matter. We asked about this and were told the United States was paying for the separate USO facilities. Our own government was making this possible. All our guys wanted were a coke and a hot dog. No big deal, right? Wrong."

"While we were fighting Nazi Germany and Japan and their versions of racial superiority."

"One of the paradoxes of the war. Black sailors fighting racist regimes, while their own people mistreated them…"

"I never really came to terms with that stuff. Just struck me as wrong."

"My sentiments exactly."

The two men pondered what had been said and what could not be undone.

"Eric, to make a point, the disease found us in Charleston Harbor. Twice…"

"South Carolina…"

"Focus of the slave trade… In fact, the center of the hideous commerce… People in bondage… Families split up… The whip lashing strong backs… Human beings checked out as if they were prime horses. The first shots of the Civil War were fired here. Old Fort Sumter… But that's in the past. We were tied up with three other ships on the outermost side. For our sailors to get to the pier, they had to cross three DEs. As they did, derogatory remarks were made, such as 'He's from the nigger ship. He's from the Black ship.' Or 'Here come the coons.' I instructed the men to pay no attention. To just walk right by the knuckleheads."

"Did they?"

"They were disciplined. They knew what was at stake. They couldn't win fighting words. I'm sure your men knew that, too."

"Indeed. We talked about it a lot. What about the other incident?"

"USO girls came aboard the Mason to dance on the fantail. They had done this with other ships birthed with us. The white shipyard workers tried to charge up the gangplank and take the girls off. I had our men man at battle stations. We turned our guns on the troublemakers. They backed off. I think our crew would have handled these guys even without weapons."

"Bill, I have no doubt."

"Looks like both crews went through a lot."

"Even when it came to training. Hard to believe but true… Permit me to explain. Very early in the war, the Navy learned that too many sailors were dying after their ships had been torpedoed. Not from the initial blast... Our men didn't know how to abandon ship in a proper manner, or how to swim through water where there was burning oil. To improve the survival rate, the Navy required all crews of submarine chasers to go through special training, which was held at Miami Beach."

"I'm afraid I know what's coming."

"A tower was constructed at the end of a pier. It had a platform approximating the height of a PC's top deck. Each sailor was shown how to jump from the platform before he did it. He was also taught how to save a drowning shipmate, and how to perform artificial respiration."

"What happened, Eric?"

"Our training and practice was cancelled. The Miami Beach city government refused the use of its public beach for the training of Negroes. The Navy accepted the city's position. In 1944, all military bases within the United States adhered to local customs and attitudes. There was no legal recourse, or so the government said."

"And I thought there was a war going on."

"Two wars, I think. One to defeat the Axis Powers... The other at home, either to defend or overturn our legacy of racial segregation."

"Not much we could do about it."

"Just captain our ships."

"And our crews."

SEGREGATED USO IN THE SOUTH

—————————————

I sat back. I turned off the computer. I even saved what I had written. It pays to leave a big print message on the computer: SAVE ME. Beats anything on the screen, especially when you're dog-tired. And I was. The Captains were getting to me. It was almost as if they were in charge, directing my thoughts, manipulating my fingers on the keyboard. For a moment, I wondered who was writing their story?

The contradictions were getting to me. America at war, abroad and at home… The Navy's experiment — ending segregation in the service by creating two Black crews, segregated from white sailors… Ask our youth to fight in our name, yet refuse them a hot dog and coke because of color. Then there was Mary Berkeley Minor Blackford, and her husband, William Matthew Blackford, who owned slaves but tried to effect their liberation by sending them back to Africa, while the good folks of Miami Beach wouldn't let Black sailors train on their beaches. And finally, there was Ireland. Catholic… White… Distant… Who would have guessed what would happen when the USS Mason docked in the land of leprechauns?

I clicked back on my computer. Time to finish a thought.

"Bill, you got to Ireland. The 1264 got to Cuba. Funny thing, though, we were often treated better outside of the old USA than inside."

"July 1944… We arrived in Belfast after leaving Bangor Harbor. I knew the crew was apprehensive. After all, 160 Black sailors were about to descend on the white population. As always, I told my crew to stay together, don't go alone. And mind your manners."

"Good advice."

"Turns out it wasn't needed. The friendly Irish greeted our guys with open arms, big smiles, and friendship. Our crew had never been treated that way by perfect strangers, certainly not in Dixie… I was curious. For many of my crew, they had to travel across the Atlantic to be treated like human beings. It was a sense of being liberated many of the crew told me, something they had never experienced before. Who could blame our Black sailors for thinking that way, since back home they had to sit in the Negro section of the theater, or weren't permitted to sit down at a Woolworth counter?"

"The Irish came through."

"Didn't they, Eric? The Irish people weren't put off by skin color. They looked at my crew as Americans, Navy fighting men. Of course, they weren't above playing a few jokes on their temporary guests."

"Oh."

"As I heard the story, four of our sailors went on a tour of the city. After it ended, the guide offered to have beers with the men. The barman provided pints of beer, which the men quickly downed. Only the beer was warm, and the men spat it up on the floor as the Irish watched gleefully."

"A good laugh was had by all."

"And it was nice to be accepted as 'Yanks.' Not Black sailors. Just Yanks."

"Bill, tell me about the reporter on the Mason."

"You know about Young, Thomas W.?"

"Navy scuttlebutt."

"Thanks to that guy, the Negro press published information about the 'experiment.' His family owned the Journal and Guide of Norfolk, Virginia. The paper was the largest Black employer in the South during the war. It also had a circulation of over 100,000 and carried a national edition. I later learned it won four Wendell Wilkie awards for outstanding journalism. It informed the Negro community on events and issues of interest to them, including housing and job discrimination, and how Blacks were doing in the services.

Thomas W. Young was the first Black war correspondent to report from a U.S. Navy warship. His articles were reproduced by Black newspapers in every American city. He tended to focus on individuals, their duties, and the family life aboard the Mason. Yet, he also narrowed in on the importance of 'Eleanor's Folly.' One of his headlines ran, 'The USS Mason Goes to War — History is Made.'"

THE REPORTER

"We never had a reporter on the 1264. Just at portside."
"Missed out, I'm afraid. At least with Young… He even put in a kind word for me in one dispatch. He said:"

'The crew of the Mason wants to make good, and from my observations, it is entirely capable of doing so. One fortunate circumstance, it seems to me, is the further fact that they have a thoroughly competent Commanding Officer, who has won both the confidence and admiration of the men.'

"An endorsement from the press… I would have liked that."
"I tried not to let it go to my head. Young captured the emotions of GQ in one of his articles that did play well with the folks back home."

"The first General Quarters alarm was sounded our very first day at sea. This was the call to arms, the sobering warning that these Negro-rated men and specialists were at last really in the war as part of Uncle Sam's fighting Navy.

A GQ is a tense, exciting experience, no matter how many you've been through before. You may be sleeping, or eating, or playing cards… When the gong begins to ring and a voice on the public address system sternly orders, 'All hands, man your battle stations' — well, you tingle just a little bit inside because you don't know how far away the enemy is or in what strength he will strike."

"That gong still makes me tingle, Bill."
"Right up the spine."
"Did Young know about the experiment? Write about it?"
"Did he ever."

"The Navy sent the Mason out here to do a fighting job, nothing more. But because it drew on white chief petty officers and a few white-rated men with prior experience on warships to complement the crew, the Navy also created, no doubt entirely without design, a proving ground or floating laboratory.

Here is being tested the ability of its men in uniform to live and work peacefully and harmoniously and effectively, irrespective of previously applied patterns of separation. Here is being produced the evidence that 'Americans of all backgrounds and all complexions can and will settle down to the business of fighting together against a common enemy.'"

"He captured the moment, Bill. No question about that."

"Did well by his father, P.B. Young, Senior. I think the old man pushed his son to join the Mason. He knew a good story. He relied on quiet, factual journalism rather than 'sensationalism.' Also, he kept the paper moderate, certainly less militant than other Black papers in the North. But he certainly got the story right about this destroyer escort."

Much can be said about the Captains. What can be said of one was equally true of the other. For each, the following was true:

As long as you do your job, what your rank calls for, you'll have no problem. I'm just here to run a U.S. Navy ship. I am not here to solve any race problems.

Or:

"He acted toward us as man to man. We all thought he was a great man. He understood human nature. He didn't treat anyone as an inferior."

As for the Captains, their respect and admiration for their crews was straightforward and deserving:

"Am delighted with the colored men who are here. They know what they are doing and really put out the work... I think the crew is better than average... They are anxious to make a name for themselves and actually work harder."

It was time for the captains to depart. They had done their duty. No more could be asked of them. As they faded from my consciousness, a few lines of a John Masefield poem came to mind:

I must go down to the seas again, to the lonely sea and the sky,
And all I ask is a tall ship and a star to steer her by,
And the wheel's kick and the wind's song and the white sail's shaking,
And a gray mist on the sea's face, and a gray dawn breaking...

Gray dawn breaking... I knew with absolute certainty where the story now went. The clang of the gong now beckoned me. The clash of arms was in the air. Born to do battle, the two ships, the USS Mason and PC 1264, must now claim their birthright. In my head, I heard the words resounding through both ships:

"Man your battle stations…"

CHAPTER 19

TORPEDO JUNCTION

<u>TWO WEEKS LATER – SEATTLE</u>

" Garvey, look at you. No pile of dusty, old documents in front of you. No computer screen I can detect. Just you and a large root beer float and the remains of that giant, double cheeseburger you ordered."

"You didn't mention the extra portion of French fries I devoured."

"I was being sensitive on your behalf."

"I had an enormous appetite today. Unusual for me... Anyway I needed to feel the sun's rays, Evelyn."

"I agree. You were looking a little wan. You needed to get some color."

For a moment we just gazed at each other. Then, as if rehearsed, we burst into a rich laugh, loud and long, which brought stares from other Washington students in the quad area near the Student Union Building. It took them a moment to gather our rampaging wits --- that is, to control the avalanche of funny sensations rolling through them.

"You think I need color, Evelyn?"

"Not according to your DNA --- WASP-looking dad married to a beautiful Polynesian-looking woman, whose father was Black, and who in turn married a very light-complexioned-white woman."

"Yeah, that's me, halves and quarters, my DNA gone wild. Now, what about you?"

"Garvey, you already know about my background --- Chinese mother who married a dark-skinned man from Colombia."

"Maybe that's why you like tacos with your pork fried rice?"

"Perhaps… We are quite a pair, aren't we?"

Of course, the answer was yes. In more ways than one… Since they went to a dance together, they had been a developing item, enjoying each other's company, spending what time they could with each other, but never interfering with the need to hit the books, or write a thesis. Very sensible, if not uncharacteristic of young love on a college campus… Romance was in the air. Garvey knew it, as did Evelyn. It was coming along slow and steady. In short, no white water was rushing them headlong downstream. And that was okay with them and families, who could tell something was in the air. Parents, it seemed, have a genetic-radar for these sorts of things.

As for Evelyn's DNA… She had beautiful almond-shaped eyes and a bronze-hue to her skin. The combo was irresistible. Notwithstanding his school obligations, plus his teaching responsibilities, and the pull of research, Garvey wanted to spend what time was left over with Evelyn. That appears to be what pangs of the heart are all about.

"Anyway, the sun feels good, genetic inheritance or not, Evelyn."

"Well, watch out. You can still get a sunburn."

"That's why I put *Sea and Ski 3,000* on. Covered myself in white paste."

"I'll let that one pass, Garvey. So, what are you working on today besides the float?

"Torpedo Junction."

"Naturally. It's a quite common topic on campus."

"Could be if you are 're from North Carolina."

"Because?"

"They might know about Cape Hatteras."

"Since I don't, you'll explain?"

"You really want to know?"

"Of course. Your research is of great interest to me, more than you can possibly imagine."

"It all has to do with *PC 1264*."

———————————

Evelyn's comment --- "more than you can possibly imagine" --- struck a responsive nerve. What was she getting at? What was the "more?" What unknown "something" lay behind the pleasant face and the seemingly innocent words? Questions... No answers... Perhaps in time...

———————————

"If Pearl Harbor caught the nation by surprise, Torpedo Junction caught the Navy off guard and ill-prepared to deal with the earliest and greatest threat to America's security at the beginning of the war, the German U-boat campaign off our eastern seaboard. In the immediate days of the war after war was declared, Hitler unleashed a secret plan, code-named *Operation Drumroll*. His idea was for submarines to creep into local American waters and wreak havoc on defenseless merchant ships carrying cargo and fuel.

THE U-BOAT MENACE

And this they did. In a six-month period—from January to June 1942—some 397 ships were sunk just off the North Carolina coast alone. The situation was so dire that captains began calling the area "Torpedo Junction." It was here that the slaughter began, pitting lurking submarines against slow-moving merchant ships.

TORPEDOED MERCHANT SHIP

––––––––––––

"How awful." "And unnecessarily tragic." "You'll explain."

"It was said, Evelyn, that you could read a newspaper by the glow at night from flaming tankers burning just offshore. As for the beaches, the morning tides washed ashore the flotsam and jetsam of torpedoed merchant ships—oil, wreckage, and bodies. The signs of war were strewn across the Carolina coast.

"Believe it or not, people actually reclined in beach chairs to watch 'the show' each night. Sort of like it was a Hollywood production… They had no need for newsreels. They saw the actual, real-time footage. Amazing…

"For a while, we had only ourselves to blame for the German successes, who took advantage of our poor preparations for war. For almost a year, the Germans were able to operate with little fear of retaliation.

"At first, there was no convoy system. Ships, independent of each other, traveled along the coast as they pleased, one at a time, with—would you believe it—their running lights on? Mostly alone, they compounded their situation by cruising in a straight line rather than following a zigzag course, which made it more difficult to evade a torpedo attack. What were they thinking? Any isolated, slowly moving, lonely merchant ship was a 'sitting duck.'

"And onshore, there was equal stupidity. There were no blackout restrictions. The local Chamber of Commerce didn't want to scare away tourists. The hotels were lit up like Christmas trees. The resorts played radios, making lots of noise, giving the sub commanders a beacon to navigate by. Talk about playing into the hands of the enemy. We all but invited the nautical nightmare.

"Coastal lights in particular provided a brilliant backdrop for passing ships, which were silhouetted and easily spotted by a periscope knifing through the waters of the Atlantic. Add to that... Lighthouses and navigational buoys remained lit. Last but not least, there were not enough naval ships to protect the merchant fleet. Nor was there much in the way of patrol aircraft. Only one Coast Guard ship was available most of the time, the USS Dione. It was no match against the tested Germans."

"Tourism before ship security, Garvey?" "The transition to wartime necessity was difficult for many, especially where the dollar was involved." "To sit and watch..." "Not too different from television coverage of violence today. We sit and watch." "But this was war."

I let that comment pass. No good answer anyway. Violence took many forms—a civil war here, a terrorist bomb there, a bank robbery somewhere... Armies, gangs... Isolated and lonely individuals with an armory in the basement... National grievances, the need for revenge... All part of the same mix... Not too different from '42.

"The carnage at sea, Evelyn, did not go unnoticed by George Marshall, the Army Chief of Staff. He wrote to Admiral King on June 19, 1942."

The losses by submarines off our Atlantic seaboard and in the Caribbean now threaten our entire war effort... I am fearful that another month or two of this will so cripple our means of transport that we will be unable to bring sufficient men and planes to bear against the enemy in critical theaters to exercise a determining influence on the war.

"The urgency of the situation was beginning to hit home. Over time, the crisis required the inauguration of a coastal convoy system. Zigzag patterns were required. Long-range aircraft patrols commenced as planes and pilots were made available. And finally, and necessarily, the anti-sub chasers, destroyer escorts, and patrol craft were deployed to relieve the Coast Guard. The squeeze was on. In time, the sea would be a dangerous graveyard for the U-boats. In time..."

"And, Garvey, that's where the PC 1264 comes in?" "Exactly. By 1944, the German menace off our immediate shores had greatly reduced. But not completely... Convoys still needed protection. Patrol crafts, in particular, were still necessary to ward off a still-dangerous submarine. The 1264s were built for that sole purpose—to hunt down and destroy enemy submarines." "When we were talking yesterday, you mentioned a paradox, Garvey, something the Captain had to deal with." "Captain Eric Sinclair Purdon was caught between the proverbial rock and a hard place. On the one hand, taking a ship into harm's way was always a dangerous proposition. Certainly, successfully dealing with the enemy was good for reputations, advancement, and the war effort. Excitement attending such engagements did make the blood flow and gave way later to a retelling of heroics, which often bordered on hyperbole. On the other hand, not dealing with the enemy led to boredom and mere repetition of actions in a rote-like manner. A lack of coming to grips with the foe was not good for ship morale. This led to a real quandary for the Captain." "Which was?" "Convoy duty was okay. A necessity. Nothing to be disparaged... However, serious allegations had been made about what the reactions would be of Black sailors under enemy shellfire. Without question, no captain relishes being a target for enemy shells, bullets, or mines, if not torpedoes. Not for a social experiment. Not for anything. But in the absence of a violent engagement, nothing definitive could be said about Black sailors in action. In short, Captain Purdon needed to get his ship into a fight." "He needed to come across a sub?" "In a nutshell, Evelyn, yes. He knew his Black crew was competent. Others knew that, too. The unknown was battle. How would his sailors measure up? Having trained and lived with the men, he had no qualms. They would conduct themselves honorably. But others needed to be convinced." "What happened?" "Frustration… Lousy welding… A conspiracy of the gods… And a lucky break… Literally…" "Okay, you have my attention, Garvey." "What do you know about the construction of a PC?" "Nothing, really. I mean, it's streamlined. It must have a motor. It's got guns. I saw that in the photographs you showed me, all those ships in the graveyard." "The ship's hull is less than ¼-inch thick. That's what stands between the crew and saltwater. Not much. The engines are below deck. Two of them, each weighing over eight tons… They're welded to heavy girders, which are attached to steel ribs of the hull. The engine room is crowded, dark, and dangerous. Following me, Evelyn?" "I think so." "The girders are called engine plates. They support the engines. They run the length of the engine room. This spreads the weight of the engines above the thin skin of the hull. Basic physics…" "Got it." "Everything depends on the welding. Three days before the 1264 was to participate in its first convoy, two motor machinist mates 2/c discovered something in the engine room." "Let me guess. There was a problem with the welding?" "Smart girl. They discovered a series of cracks running along the welds between the engine and the bedplates. They notified the Captain, who notified the base engineer. All three reached the same verdict. If the 1264 encountered unusually rough seas, the engines could shift and slide off the bedplates. They would then drop through the bottom of the ship." "No more PC 1264." "And no convoy to Key West. The ship had to go into dry dock." "Bad luck, Garvey." "Not necessarily. The missed convoy, the one PC 1264 would have shepherded to Key West before returning to base three weeks later, was a sad sight. It was the hurricane season, and the convoy ran into a fierce one that tore up the waters along the east coast. All the ships of the escort group received extensive damage. To quote the Navy:"

The small escorts were particularly battered. The torrents of water pouring over their superstructures tore away lifelines, stanchions, the ammunition-ready boxes, rafts, and even radio and radar antennae. Most tragically, the executive officer of the USS PC 1265 was swept from the bridge and lost.

"The 1264 would have been lost in that storm. No doubt about it, Evelyn. Misfortune proved a godsend in this case. Instead of resting on the bottom of the Atlantic, the ship was towed to the Navy Yard Annex in Bayonne, New Jersey. Her afterdeck was cut open, and her engines were pulled out. The entire repair job took ten weeks." "The fates are fickle, Garvey. If the cracks hadn't been discovered… If the ship had sunk… If the Black sailors had perished… What would have become of the experiment? Some would have concluded the ship sank because it had a Black crew. The color of the crew's skin would have taken the hit, not Mother Nature." "You've got that right. Even as it was, malicious rumors spread that the crew was at fault. All protests to the contrary, the crew couldn't win this argument in some quarters. People believed what they wanted. Ugly situation." "After the repairs… What happened?" "April 25, 1944… That's what happened." "Teasing me again, professor?" "A little." "If you want a float refill…" "Or a partner for the next dance?" "You're catching on fast."

The truth was, I liked to tease Evelyn a bit. Just innocent stuff about history… I'm not sure if she genuinely loved history, especially the war years, but she put up a good front and was certainly a quick study. Deep down, I think she was really interested in the fate of the Black sailors, whether on the PC 1264 or the USS Mason, and maybe something else, for all I knew. And I, of course, enjoyed being her mentor. Plus, I wanted another float. Salty seawater gives a person a real thirst.

"It was three weeks before V-E Day, May 8, 1945. German armies, sandwiched between the Russians in the east and the Allied forces in the west, were collapsing all along the fronts. It was just a matter of time. Captain Purdon's crew had little time to waste if they were going to get into a shooting war in the Atlantic. They needed a break. The

Navy granted their wish. They would be in a last convoy. But not only that… They would be the lead ship in the convoy. The 1264 would be responsible for planning and putting up an adequate anti-submarine screen for thirty ships." "Was the Navy testing the ship?" "No documents to prove that, but…" "Circumstantial evidence suggests…"

CHAPTER 20

CONVOY DUTY

"A decision was made to give the 1264 the job. And what a job it was... Three PC's to nursemaid thirty vulnerable ships in the last desperate days of the war. Any sub in the area had one last chance to loose its torpedoes. The run from Charleston Harbor to 'north of Hatteras,' then to New York Harbor, was still a dangerous stretch of water. Northward through Torpedo Junction, with pregnant tankers and freighters loaded to the gills... Talk about an easy target."

"Captain Purdon first decided on his convoy pattern. He would form a wide, rectangular box of eight columns, with four ships in each column. The 1264, the command ship, would be in front to cover the advancing line of ships. The other two PCs, the 1149 and the 1547, would screen from the starboard and port sides. In theory, it was a good plan."

"Conventional operation?"

"Nothing conventional about a multi-nation operation. Eight ships were from the British Merchant Navy. There were four Norwegian ships, one Dutch ship... and seventeen American ships. Four nations in a convoy — KN-382..."

"How far did they have to go?"

"Over 380 miles as the bird flies, at about 8 knots. Slow going. Speed was determined by the slowest ships in the convoy."

THE CONVOY

"The PCs depended on their radar and sonar, their guns, and their depth charges."

"Exactly what is a depth charge, Garvey?"

"Think of a garbage can full of explosives falling through the water with a fuse set to cause detonation at a preselected depth. The explosion subjects a submarine to a tremendous hydraulic shock, sufficient to blow rivets, opening up the sub to the sea. A direct hit is not always necessary. The 'can' just needs to detonate in the immediate area. And remember, many depth charges are fired at a sub. The combined explosions amplify the power of the underwater bombs. No sub commander wants to be near one of them. Subs hunker down as deeply as possible and run as silently as they can, staying that way until their oxygen needs to be replenished. Usually, they didn't surface unless they were severely damaged. And then they came up to fight..."

"Tedious work, convoying, and dangerous."

"True, Evelyn, but necessary with a big plus this time. When you're the lead ship, the convoy depends on you. Thirty ships depended on the

1264. Thirty ships depended on the Black crew of the 1264. For these men, things would never be the same. They had been taught skills. They were competent. They were leaders. They had met and lived with men they never knew before war brought them together. They had rubbed elbows. They had shared ideas. Made friends… They had expressed their hopes and desires. Their prewar lives would no longer suffice within the narrow confines of Jim Crow laws or unstated prejudice in other areas of the country. They had been treated like men in the Navy. They would demand the same respect in civilian life. They had changed. And they knew it. In the terrible equation of life and death in wartime, with all the destruction and pain, at least this had come out of the conflict. New men were born in the crucible of war."

"Garvey, such passion."

"I guess I see myself as one of the crew."

"Angered by Jim Crow?"

"Defiant."

"And hopeful?"

"A better world had to be possible."

"My idealist."

"Just a guy writing about the past. So let's get back to it. Tedium there was. Routine existed… Practice and more practice each day… Always training… And a growing sense of self-worth, Evelyn."

"They did get the convoy to New York, didn't they?"

"Every hour they traveled eight miles, and each day brought them closer to their destination. But fate wasn't through with the PC 1264."

"Teasing again?"

"Dramatic moment."

"Give, Garvey."

"April 28th… Saturday… The convoy was steaming northward. On the PC, emergency drills were being held to keep the crews on their toes. Over the PA… 'General Quarters… All hands man your battle stations.' The announcement aboard each ship… The signal to prepare for battle. All over each ship, crewmembers reported to their stations and prepared for action. Fireproof and watertight doors were slammed shut between bulkheads. Sailors dropped whatever they were doing, donned their battle gear, and sprinted to their assigned positions. Seconds counted."

BATTLE STATIONS

"You're milking this, Garvey."

"The convoy was past Hatteras. Some 350 miles to go… Convoy's course, 352 degrees… Last leg of the journey… It was Sunday, April 29, 1945… History would be made this day."

"Still toying."

"Give a guy a break. I'm doing this without my notes."

"And enjoying every moment."

It was true. I was enjoying myself. I knew the story by heart. I didn't need notes.

"Evelyn, this story takes time. Bear with me."

"Oh, I am."

"Late on the night of April 29th, Captain Purdon, using his sextant, took a number of star sights in order to get a fix. Quickly, he computed his numbers. It had been a good shot. He knew his position and that of the convoy. They were on schedule. He marked the chart and then projected where the convoy would be at 9:30 P.M. the next day. At that point on the chart, he then wrote 'SS,' the abbreviation for a submarine, to see if his XO would notice the marking, indicating what had not happened yet."

"The Captain was enjoying himself. Testing his officer, sure. Pulling a gag, yes. The XO saw the notification and called the Captain's attention to it. In turn, the Captain erased the marking on the chart, saying, 'I've just killed him.' The executive officer knew he had been had at that point."

"The next day at precisely 9:30 A.M., plus five minutes, a German submarine did appear on the course line of the convoy. Who could have predicted that? It was the U-548, a 750-ton snorkel-fitted undersea boat. The word went out to the convoy, 'Submarine sighted off port bow.' The PCs attacked. Depth charge detonations rolled toward the convoy, which made a 45-degree course change away from the periscope sighting. The sub, now under attack, dove for the bottom."

"Questions lingered. Why had the sub surfaced so close to the convoy and its lethal escorts? It made no sense. Why hadn't it just attacked? Then the Captain realized the awful truth. The sub had surfaced to drive the convoy in another direction. Allied antisubmarine doctrine required a 45-degree turn away from the German U-boat. The convoy was possibly moving directly toward a waiting Wolf Pack. As the Captain was considering this, the radar room notified the Captain:

'Targets bearing dead ahead. Range seven miles and closing at 14 knots.' The bogies were 15 minutes away."

"The PC 1264 had the honor of intercepting the bogies. Gun crews were alerted for imminent surface action. The ship was no longer patrolling. She was headed directly toward the oncoming targets."

"Had this been a Hollywood script, grand music would have been heard in the background. Men at the guns would have been seen in close-ups. Depth charges would be exploding, throwing up huge spouts of water. The Captain on the bridge would be seen peering through his night glasses. A white captain, a Black crew…"

But this wasn't Hollywood…

"The Captain ordered, 'Challenge them.' A signal lamp was used to show the letter A, the single-letter challenge for that segment of the day. Those with binoculars strained to see what the answer would be. Six thousand yards… Three and a quarter miles… The three blips grew larger. Too big for submarines… But, what were they? Then came the correct signal reply… Q for Queen. Friendly ships…"

"Task Group 02.10, a hunter-killer group, was on the prowl for any Nazi sub still off the coast. The group was composed of three destroyers — the USS Thomas, USS Coffman, and USS Bostwick. Passing by the 1264, the destroyers went after the U-548, which tried every trick to avoid the pursuers. It was to no avail. Depth charges were dropped, followed by heavy explosions and the sound of the submarine breaking up and oil floating to the surface. Fifty-eight men died. There were no survivors. This turned out to be the last submarine action in the Atlantic."

"As for the 1264, she caught up with the convoy and led it to its destination. A few days later, Germany surrendered. The war in Europe was over. The war in the Pacific still raged."

"Every sailor on the PC 1264 had proven his competency and dedication to duty. Though no shots had been fired at the ship, the crew had acquitted itself in the best traditions of the United States Navy. For the men, the officers, and the captain, there was no question about this. The experiment had disproved old views and tired attitudes."

"That's some story, Garvey."

"I thought so."

"It struck me that you — had you been alive at the time — might have been a part of the experiment."

"And unable to get a hot dog and coke in the local drugstore, Evelyn."

"And I wouldn't have, as a woman, been on a naval ship as a sailor."

"This man's navy is proud to have you aboard today."

"What's next, Garvey?"

"The USS Mason in the North Atlantic. Want to hear that story?"

"Does the UW Huskie like purple?"

CHAPTER 21

THE NORTH ATLANTIC

A FEW HOURS LATER – SEATTLE

Evelyn would be back in a few minutes. Okay, two hours… She needed to meet with her adviser and do a couple of household chores. As to what they were, I was not informed. And that's how I found myself with a little time on my hands, which I could use to collect my thoughts. Translated, that meant I had a moment to think about Evelyn and what was happening. Exposition… What was happening meant our relationship. Somewhere… Perhaps in the back of my mind… Whatever that was supposed to mean… I knew our relationship was getting serious. It wasn't that I was opposed to that. Rather, I wondered if I was ready for it. You know, commitments and that sort of thing. I knew I was infatuated with Evelyn. But did that mean I loved her? I knew I missed her when she wasn't around. But was I ready to consider vows?

I needed help.

"Gramps, you around?"
"Always within earshot, Garvey."
"What've you been doing?"
"Practicing my curmudgeon skills. Trying to maintain my surly attitude."
"I'll let that pass. Gramps, I've met a girl."
"I know."

"You do?"

"You dream a lot. And you talk in your sleep."

"She's beautiful."

"Naturally."

"I think I'm in love."

"Think or know?"

"Something in between."

"Figures. Most guys go through this. Happened to me with your grandmother."

"Really?"

"You think you're the first guy to get cold feet? Sweaty palms? Lightheadedness? Dry mouth? And…"

"Stop there, Gramps. I'm beginning to feel like a physiological disaster."

"Not to worry."

"There's a way out?"

"Just give in. Admit it, life with Evelyn is better than life without her."

"How did you know her name?"

"Your heart keeps pounding out in Morse Code — E-V-E-L-Y-N."

"You spy on me?"

"Never. I merely hang around taking in the world."

"You are spying on me."

"Let's leave it at this. I take an interest in you."

Gramps was always one step ahead of me. I guess almost getting to a hundred gives you an edge. I wondered if I should ask him what else was behind my mental torment?

Weighing the few options open to me, I decided to seek counsel.

"Gramps, what should I do?"

"If it was me, Garvey, I wouldn't let this beauty get away. She's cool."

"She is, isn't she?"

"So just get over your qualms. Take a chance on life, Garvey. You can't spend your whole life on this thesis. Kick it in the backside and move on."

"Not easy."

"Didn't say it was, Garvey."

"No other advice?"

Before Gramps could answer, Evelyn returned. My time for reflection was over, at least outwardly. Bouncing back into my life, Evelyn said with a big smile, "I'm ready to hear about the Mason."

For a moment I couldn't speak. Some cat had gotten my tongue. I just looked at her, a quizzical look on my face. Maybe a stupid one...

"Something wrong, Garvey?"

I couldn't say anything about my conversation with Gramps, the ghost of my past and present life. So I did the only thing I could. I punted. I changed the topic.

"Everything work out okay with your adviser?"

"Got a complete go-ahead on my thesis topic. My M.A. beckons."

"Which is?"

"The war years."

"Big topic."

"A tiny slice, which I will tell you about in time."

I fought back the need to know. Why that was important to me, I couldn't quite understand. It was time to punt again.

"Evelyn..."

"Yes?"

"After I complete my thesis, I want to ask you a question."

I blurted out the words. I'm not sure what I expected.

"Sure. And I have a question for you..."

"Really? What is it?"

"When your doctoral work is done."

Now I was in a real tizzy. What was her question? I still had a few months to go before I was finished with the research. How could I wait that long? And then more time with my committee when it reviewed the final thesis. God, I'd never last. As for Evelyn, she didn't seem to have these concerns about my question. Did she already know? Did she suspect? Had Gramps been talking to her?

"Garvey, speak. Tell me about the Mason and what happened in the North Atlantic."

"The story of the USS Mason in 1945 is the stuff of legend, heroics, and disappointment. It could easily be entitled, The Battle of the Barges, or, for those who want a more negative connotation, The Unkindest Cut. The choice is yours to make.

"Convoy NY-199 began its trek across the Atlantic, some 50 ships strong with an unusual array of vessels — common merchant ships, and an uncommon fleet of bulky Army tugs pulling massive, but leaky car floats some 3,539 miles across the wildest, most dangerous seas to England — the North Atlantic, known for its fierce storms, gusting winds, and towering waves. In addition, the USS Maumee, an oil tanker, went along for the ride. She was a floating gas station. All the ships and tugboats would need to refuel at sea, always a challenging proposition given the few lurking German subs still at sea. Around the fleet would be the ubiquitous destroyer escorts, providing a protective shield.

"Commander Alfred L. Lind was in charge of the armada, Task Group 27.5, such as it was. He was stationed on the Maumee. He was an experienced seaman, but nothing in his experience prepared him for what was about to happen."

USS MAUMEE

CAPTAIN LIND

"The convoy, if not doomed from the start, was at least in jeopardy from the word go. It was more than snakebitten. On this point, naval historians are in agreement."

First came the realization that many of the smaller craft had an incredible number of mechanical shortcomings for a transatlantic trip. Then came the impact of not having enough qualified sailors to operate the tugs. The crews had no deep-sea sailing experience. The 14 railroad car floats (barges), some 250 feet long and carrying a 60-ton crane, should never have been put to sea. They were simply too big, ungainly, and heavy to tow across the open ocean.

"The ships could only average 4.74 miles per hour. Why so slow? Simply put, the tugs were pulling barges once used to ferry railroad cars across New York Harbor. The barges were underpowered. They were sometimes referred to as car floats. They had rail tracks mounted on the deck and could carry eight to ten railroad cars at a time, an immense load. Approximately 250 to 360 feet long and 45 feet wide, these barges were designed for short hauls — to be tugged along beside a tugboat for a 30-minute trip across New York Harbor. Even in relatively placid water, they were difficult to maneuver, whether pushed or towed. They were prone to flipping around, a result of their weight. Heavily timbered and constructed with at least 30% iron, they were almost unsinkable. Why was this? The answer: These barges were built with twelve separate, nearly watertight compartments."

CAR FLOATS

"The question arises: why were these barges being towed to England? It was assumed they would make excellent temporary piers on the Normandy coast following D-Day. This view was most espoused by Admiral Eugene Moran, formerly of the Moran Tugboat Co. He was not without experience. He had commanded an armada of tugs and barges that spent ten days ferrying concrete caissons and steel piers across the English Channel to establish man-made harbors immediately after June 6th. He was a man who knew his business. But crossing the Channel was far different than crossing the Atlantic.

"Part of the problem lay with the Army tugboats. The crews were generally inexperienced with blue-water sailing, and the people on the tugs knew little about their engines. In some cases, due to high winds and tides, they lost their fresh water supply and most of their food. Seasickness hit them hard. They were used to being on land. A few were even thrown overboard. The convoy had to stop to pick up those in the water. The tugs were always floundering with their towed barges. They constantly needed to regroup within the convoy.

"For the first 20 days of the trip to England, the waves were moderate — only ten feet high with winds of 20 miles per hour, all normal for the Atlantic that late in the year — 1944. Then the storms hit. From October 10th through the 23rd, the winds picked up, reaching as high as 40 mph with gusts up to 90 miles per hour. Forty to fifty-foot waves pounded the fleet.

"In such seas, the inevitable occurred. The barges swung wildly from the tugboats, fraying the holding lines and capsizing three tugboats. Eight steel car floats sank, along with five cargo barges. Nineteen men lost their lives."

ROUGH WEATHER

Here's the refined version of the passage for better flow and clarity:

"In the war diary of the Mason, Yeoman Mel Grant wrote terse comments:

Screening starboard bow as before. Wind and sea rising. Many breakdowns reported by small craft and increasing difficulty with tow wires… Some alarm noted in TBS (talk between ships) transmissions. Ships rolling in the storms.

"Even the destroyer escorts were at risk. Hastily built as 'throw-away ships,' they were considered temporary vessels, used exclusively for convoy duty and to hunt down submarines. They were fast, powerfully armed, but not designed to take this kind of punishment. They were constantly rolling and pitching, going up and down. Seawater continuously flowed over the bow. It was so cold that when water hit the steel deck, it turned immediately to ice. Ship lines (ropes) were two inches thick with ice. Sailors used them on the slippery deck to avoid slipping overboard as the ship heaved its way through mountainous waves. But when seawater hit the lines, ice built up on them, reaching three to four inches thick. Frozen lines were of little use to the crew.

"One false move on the slick deck meant being thrown overboard. Unless you drowned, you froze to death within a few minutes. The North Atlantic was unforgiving — a natural 'torpedo alley.'

"Inside the wheelhouse of the Mason was an incline meter. It had a very special function. It measured the degree to which a ship had rolled. It's like a pendulum on a clock, with a graduated scale. Degrees are measured from dead center all the way up to ninety."

INCLINE METER

"Most sailors, if they have experienced a 40-degree roll, are apt to brag about surviving it. Anything greater can topple a ship, rolling it so far that it cannot return to an even keel. A 90-degree roll means the ship is flat on its side.

"In October, the weather turned bad. The worst possible conditions prevailed. Winds hit 75 miles per hour, and the seas heaved higher and higher.

"The huge wave that struck the Mason caught it almost broadside. The ship rolled past 40 degrees, 50 degrees, and 60 degrees, all the way to 70 degrees. Seawater nearly obliterated the ship. The radio room took in water. Equipment had to be covered to keep water out of the electrical components. The antenna tower of the ship broke apart and had to be hastily repaired. Twenty-one inches of water collected in the chain lockers."

70-DEGREE ROLL

"For a time, it seemed the Mason would fall apart at its seams and sink. The nonstop pounding topside was almost too much for the ship. Cracks developed that the repair crews had to weld. Some compartments buckled and needed shoring up.

"A destroyer escort is about twelve feet wide. It is very small. It rides high on the water, light and bouncy, like a wild horse, up and down. It doesn't take much water to cover it.

"The Mason was swamped. The wave that hit the ship poured water down into the decks below, and worst of all, into the engine room, where the crew scrambled to cover their switchboard with canvas to keep the water from reaching the electricity.

"It was a general understanding in the Navy that a ship doesn't survive such a roll — 70 degrees or more. The Mason, however, rolled and rolled, then held, lurched, and finally came back. Lorenzo DuFau recalled that moment years later, adding some perspective."

"The actual experience of having a storm hit a convoy made us realize just how small man was on that ocean, how small the ships were in comparison. Our ship, our destroyer escort, would be caught in the trough at the bottom of a wave, then taken up to the top. We stood at the crest for a moment, then descended like a kid sliding down a slide. That was the most frightening experience, to realize we were out in an ocean acting up that way, and we had so little control over the ship. We were almost at its mercy, trying to steer that ship into the sea to maintain some headway and keep a semblance of control."

LISTING

———————————————

"Garvey, I can't imagine what it was like… You know, being at sea in a storm like that. And almost rolling over… I almost lost my burger when you told me about that."

"It's fair to say that the worst was still to come."

"I can't believe that."

"On October 18th, the commander of NY-119 had to make a difficult decision, one that ultimately would bring honor to the Mason's sailors. Admiral Lind noted that the storm had sunk two small ships and broken up all but one of the remaining tows. Numerous small, unattached craft were in 'imminent danger of also overturning and being lost.' The choice was simple, if not grave. Should the convoy stay intact and fight the storm together, or should the small crafts be detached and given the opportunity to run for it? If the latter, those ships would not have adequate escort or service protection and assistance. They would be on their own."

"Survival of the fittest, Garvey?"

"Something like that, yes. According to the Admiral's record:

After carefully weighing all the facts and with predictions of still continued increasing high seas and wind, it was decided to send the 20 unattached small craft now in charge of the USS Mason."

"The Mason would lead them to Plymouth — the oilers, the independent tugs, and two British ships. Once this was done, the destroyer escort would head back to the fleet to assist the convoy's remaining ships. It all sounded so straightforward. On October 19th, Bishop Rock was sighted. The wind was forty knots, with gusts over fifty mph. It was difficult to get the ships into port. No one had charts of the immediate area. It was necessary for the Mason to lead the ships from buoy to buoy and between buoys. The Mason also had to run back to the rear of the column, about seven miles astern, to bring in stragglers."

"All of this would have been difficult by itself. But still another problem appeared in the least expected way. Within sight of the shoreline, the deck of the Mason broke in two."

"Garvey, you're putting me on."
"The Mason was breaking up."
"How could that be? From a torpedo hit? Bombs...? Enemy planes? Naval gunfire from German ships...?"
"None of the above."
"What then?"
"Something homemade, so to speak."

"The welding seam along the deck gave way, and it started to come apart. Reinforcing beams below deck began to collapse. Unless emergency repairs could be made, the ship was in mortal danger."

"Repairs began immediately against a frozen, sunlit sky. They continued at night in the face of fierce wind and freezing temperatures. The repair crew braved a slippery and cracking deck to make repairs. Welding under these conditions was nearly impossible, yet it was done. Had the repairs not been done, the ship would have split right in half because of the rocking and pounding of the waves. Those were brave men who made the repairs."

"The war diary of the ship took the incident in stride."

The ship handled well at all times and showed little tendency to breach running before the sea, which was by then quite high. Wind reached a maximum of seventy to eighty knots... All vessels of the advance were successfully turned over to the local escort inside the bay.

"Welding again, Garvey."
"Ironic, wasn't it?"
"Low bidder?"
"Monday riveters!"
"But at least the ship was safe in the harbor."

"For two hours, yes."

CHAPTER 22

COMMAND DECISION

"Captain Blackford made the decision to improve the welding repairs, pump out the engine room, and rig a new antenna. That took a few hours. Then the Mason put out to sea to aid the convoy still floundering in the heavy weather. Blackford requested assistance from the British. Two ships were to accompany him, the HMS Rochester and the HMS Saladin. After refueling, the ships left port together. However, almost immediately the British ships returned to port, stating that the seas were too dangerous. The Mason's crew couldn't believe it. The famous Royal Navy was turning back. What kind of sailors were they?

"The Mason had crossed the Atlantic, braving every storm, and the British couldn't help?

"The Mason's crew felt great pride. They were determined to get the job done. It took three more days at sea to complete the self-imposed responsibility.

"Admiral Lind noted the Mason's actions in his daily report concerning the incident."

The British ships refused to proceed further and returned to anchorage. The plucky USS Mason, although already damaged to the extent of having several welded seams open in her decks, effected emergency repairs and persisted in continuing to rejoin the convoy. I consider the performance of the USS Mason, her Commanding Officer, Officers, and men outstanding and recommend that this ship be given a letter of commendation to be filed in the record of each officer and man on board that vessel.

"Captain Blackford also requested that the crew of the ship be given a letter of commendation. He posted his letter on the ship's bulletin board. Certainly, the crew was proud. High seas be damned. They (the crew) had not flinched. Oliver Hazard Perry was somewhere saluting the Mason.

"The recommendation should have been the highlight of the ship's actions. The crew and its honors should have made the front pages of every Negro paper in the country, stroking Black pride throughout the country. The headlines should have screamed --- BLACK NAVY BLUEJACKETS HEROES!

"It never happened. The Navy did not follow up on the Admiral's recommendation, nor did it respond to Captain Blackford. The recommendations just disappeared. Were they lost in channels? Was there bureaucratic fumbling? Or was it something else, something akin to institutional racism…?

"It would be almost fifty years before the Admiral's letter would be found in the Navy's archives. Only then would the gallant ship and crew be recognized.

"Today the consensus by naval historians is that the Mason 'was a happy ship.' What few problems occurred were within the 'norm' for a naval vessel in terms of discipline. In short, her crew was no different than any other white crew with respect to frequency of disciplinary incidents. One unusual problem related to Black and white enlisted men from the South concerned better enunciation when using the ship's intercom system. Southern dialects were difficult for the guys from the North and West.

"As to how the men would react under stress, the Mason's crew did not differ from other crews, especially when the menace was the sea itself. By way of example, on October 18, 1944, the NY 119 was hit by the worst of the storm battering the convoy. Winds gusted to 90 mph and the seas were estimated to be fifty feet or more in height. White or Black, every sailor felt fear and was consumed by one overpowering thought: survival. However fatigued a man was, or seasick, perhaps irritated, all he wanted to do was outlast the storm and go home.

"As to other dangers, real or illusionary…"

"Some explanation, Garvey."

"Sometimes the deadly game of war can almost be comical."

"You're joking, certainly?"

"Humor is no joke in war, Evelyn."

"I fail to see the levity."

"You will."

"On October 13, 1944, one of the wooden barges broke loose from its towline and, along with a half-sunk car float. Each would be a danger to shipping. The two menaces needed to be sunk. The forward gun batteries of the USS O'Toole and the Mason were trained on the car float and firing commenced. In short order, a number of hits sank the car float. It disappeared beneath the waves.

"Now only the wooden barge was left to deal with modern gunnery and highly trained crews with extensive practice firing at towed screens and floats with 3-inch naval guns, 40 mm and 20 mm rapid-fire cannons. The barge rode ten feet above water. A visible and easy target, even if from the rough neighborhoods of the East Coast, and more to the point, New York Harbor.

"The O'Toole and the Mason jockeyed for position at a 2,000-yard range, each seeking credit for sinking the barge. The gunners warmed to their competitive task. A torrent of 3-inch shells screamed away from the ships, blasting the barge with hit after hit, but not sinking the hardy little vessel. The two ships moved closer, within 1,000 yards, and fired away with exceptional precision. Both crews, one Black, the other white, switched from armor-piercing shells to shells with explosive heads. Again, accuracy was acute. The stubborn little barge absorbed explosion after explosion, reeled slightly, but still defiantly remained afloat.

"Damaged gunnery egos were on both ships. Each ship now considered coming within 100 yards of the barge and blasting away. Any closer and the crews would have to board it, cutlasses flourishing, but an impossible task in stormy seas and a slick wooden barge frame. Instead, closer passes were made, each ship straddling the barge, and opening up with every gun available, including machine guns, Springfield rifles, and pistols. A few curses were also fired at the game little barge, which, after the smoke cleared, still remained proudly afloat.

"The situation was really getting serious. The reputation of the US Navy was at stake.

"The last effort involved depth charges. They would be dropped all around the barge, and, if possible, on the barge itself. This was done. The charges detonated. Explosions ripped the barge. The smoke cleared. The 'enemy' remained afloat. The O'Toole and the Mason struck their colors, thus ending the 'battle of the barge,' a humiliating defeat for the Bluejackets. The barge couldn't be sunk."

"Okay, Garvey, I'll grant you a modicum of satisfaction. That is a funny story. Kind of like Little Toot, the story for children."

"But only half of the story."

"What?"

"Remember, the barge alive and kicking."

"So?"

"January 11, 1945… Nighttime… Radar picked up a contact, range 2400 yards. Battle stations were ordered. Depth charges were manned. At 1500 yards, the contact was evaluated as non-sub — too many mushy echoes. Just as the crew was being secured from Battle Stations, another contact was made. A sub… No question about it. The radar indications suggested a 'remarkable resemblance to periscopes' seen during training exercises. The Captain decided to attack. Full speed ahead… At 700 yards, speed was reduced. Radar and sonar contacts held steady…

"The Mason and the contact were on a collision course. Guns were fired. Depth charges flew into the air and then into the sea. Then… Crash… The Mason struck something. The sub… It had to be the sub…

"Wreckage was seen floating in the water. Moving closer to the contact, searchlights were turned on to see the damaged sub. But there was only a wooden derelict, a barge about 150 yards long… Could it be the 'Unsinkable Dolly of Barges?'

"By computing time and normal drift, the collision occurred where the barge would be expected to be. However, you looked at it, the beat-up, shot-up, and cracked-up wooden barge with a New York attitude had the last laugh."

"You're not making all this up, Garvey?"

"Matter of naval record, log books and all that."

"Whatever happened to the barge?"

"No records. She might still be out there, flags unfurled, defying all who would mess with her timbers."

"Can we be serious for a moment, Garvey?" It just doesn't seem fair."

"That the barge beat back the barrages?"

"No. Any accomplishments by a Black unit in the services was, as you've pointed out, covered up or put on the back burner."

"Many believe the Navy — as in the Mason's case — simply did not want to give Black enlisted men credit."

"But, why?"

"If Blacks in the Navy were recognized, they might have been seen differently as a race after the war."

"You're talking about the Jim Crow laws?"

"All forms of discriminatory practices."

"An early civil rights movement, only at sea."

"Very perceptive, Evelyn. It would be almost half a century later before the story of the Mason would be made public."

"Hard to believe."

"Oh, and one other thing. When the Mason's crew went ashore in Plymouth, they went to the local USO for a hot dog and coke. Though they had braved the North Atlantic and saved British ships and sailors, the Mason's crew was told to go to the Black USO."

"Certainly, that qualifies as the final indignity. It makes me so angry."

"Stow your anger, Evelyn. The Mason's story isn't over. A last indignity awaited its crew, and that of the PC 1264, a final storm if you will."

CHAPTER 23

VICTORY

A FEW MINUTES LATER

"You have that look again, Garvey."

"I look debonair, confident, perhaps even charming and stylish?"

"Pretty smug, aren't you?"

"Merely modestly self-assured."

"Give."

"Very insistent…"

"Very."

That was true. Evelyn was now helping me with my research. She had become the extra hand I needed. Sometimes her interest in the USS Mason and the PC 1264 was so intense, almost greater than mine, as if she were on a quest of her own. I wondered about that. I mean, how many people are into something that happened 90 years ago, especially on old naval warships?

"The worst, Garvey… You promised to tell."

"A final indignity."

"Speak."

"August 6, 1945, 8:45 a.m., EST…"

"What?"

"Little Boy."

"What are you talking about, Garvey?"

"Enola Gay…"

"Fragments… How about a sentence?"

"A uranium bomb, Evelyn."

"Hiroshima?"

"Yes."

THE ATOMIC BOMB

I couldn't really blame Evelyn for being slow on that one. Most kids don't learn about the atomic bomb in school anymore. Not even in universities. It's like no one wants to recall the radioactive mushroom cloud rising over the city and the loss of life, over 100,000 killed. I mean, that's all ancient history, isn't it? And so ugly...

"11:01 a.m., August 9th, three days later..."

"The plutonium bomb?"

"'Fat Man,' Evelyn."

"Nagasaki. Another 80,000 or more dead..."

I was impressed. Evelyn's history major was clicking in. She knew her stuff, and she was about to test me.

"Okay, Garvey, August 15, 1945?"

"Easy. Japan finally surrenders."

"What about a tougher date? July 26, 1945?"

I knew the date, but I couldn't remember why. An unsettling panic began to settle in. What kind of historian was I? My pride was on the line. Make that my male pride was challenged. "Come on, Garvey," I said to myself. Calm down. Breathe easily. Don't sweat it. And smile, as if you're teasing. You can do it.

"Potsdam? President Truman's meeting with Prime Minister Churchill and Marshall Stalin of the Soviet Union?"

"Took you long enough."

"Teasing."

"I bet."

"The Potsdam Declaration?"

"Pretty good, Garvey. What was the declaration?"

"Unless Japan surrenders unconditionally, she will be subjected to 'prompt and utter destruction.'"

"And, as you pointed out to me, she was in August 1945."

"We both know what happened on August 15th, don't we, Evelyn?"

"V-J Day. Victory over Japan... The Empire surrendered."

"The bloody Pacific War was over."

"I get that, Garvey, but what does all this have to do with your research?"

"May 8, 1945 – V-E Day, the moment Germany surrendered... Victory in Europe... That's the connection."

————————————

Evelyn leaned forward, her eyes narrowing as she caught on to the subtle shift in my tone. "Not quite? What do you mean, Garvey?"

I paused, letting the weight of those words hang in the air for a moment. "Well, for the Mason, it was the end of one chapter, but not the whole story. The ship was decommissioned in 1947, as was the PC 1264, but the crew? They weren't forgotten forever."

She raised an eyebrow, a mix of curiosity and disbelief crossing her face. "So you're saying something happened after all the disappointment? After the Navy turned its back on them?"

"Yes," I said, a quiet resolve in my voice. "The Mason and its crew may have been forgotten by the public, but not by everyone. Over the years, there were whispers, small gestures of recognition, and, eventually, their story would make its way back to the surface. It just took time. Decades, even."

Evelyn leaned back, taking in the bigger picture now. "And that's what you're after, Garvey. You're telling the story they couldn't tell back then."

I nodded slowly. "Exactly. The men of the Mason and the PC 1264 had proven themselves in ways no one had expected. They were more than just sailors—they were a symbol of resilience and the fight for respect, even when it wasn't given to them. The Navy knew it. They'd been watched closely and had delivered. The crews didn't get the medals, the headlines, or the recognition they deserved, but they had their own quiet victory."

Evelyn sat in silence for a moment, her face thoughtful. "So, what happened to the men after they were decommissioned? Did they just disappear into the background of history?"

I sighed, thinking back to the next phase of their lives. "For many of them, yes. A lot went back to their communities, trying to make a living after their military service. Some left the Navy, some stayed, but opportunities for advancement were scarce. The Navy had promised them little more than being able to rise to petty officer, but nothing beyond that. Many of the men knew there was no real future for them there."

"And yet," Evelyn murmured, "they'd shown they were capable of so much more."

"That's the tragedy of it," I said. "But, even as history seemed to turn a blind eye, the Mason's legacy would slowly begin to reemerge. Not in the grand, official ceremonies we would've hoped for, but in the stories of the men themselves and in the quiet acknowledgment from those who knew better."

"Like the men who served on her, their story didn't end with decommissioning," Evelyn said softly, a bit of the weight of the narrative settling in.

"No," I agreed. "It took decades for their efforts to be recognized, and even longer for the true value of their service to be fully acknowledged in the broader historical record. But their story has its place—long after the ship was scrapped and the world moved on from the war. And, in the end, it was worth telling."

Evelyn looked at me with a deep understanding. "It's their story, Garvey. And yours, too."

I smiled slightly, grateful for her partnership in this journey. "Maybe. But I wouldn't have gotten this far without you."

CHAPTER 24

ALL HONORS

Navy Day, October 27, 1945... President Harry Truman reviewed the mighty American naval fleet—aircraft carriers, battleships, cruisers, destroyers, DEs, submarines, and a PC. The review was meant to showcase America's naval power. Forty-seven ships participated. The PC chosen for the naval review was the 1264. It was an honor well deserved.

On Wednesday, October 24th, the 1264 headed to Hampton Roads, then left the Chesapeake for the Atlantic, making its way to New York Harbor by passing through the "Narrows" and, of course, the Statue of Liberty, all the way to the Hudson River. The ship berthed at Pier 80, at the foot of West 40th Street in Manhattan.

On October 27th, at 3:30 p.m., the President boarded the USS Renshaw. At that exact moment, 3:30 p.m. on the dot, 1,200 Navy planes appeared, flying overhead in an endless V-shaped formation. It was a spectacular demonstration of naval air power.

USS RENSHAW

The 47 ships were spread out over 7 miles, from the USS Missouri at the beginning of the line to the PC 1264 at the end. As the President passed each ship, a 21-gun salute was given. The PC crew could gauge the President's progress by the sounds and puffs of gunfire, flashes, and smoke.

THE FLEET IN REVIEW   NAVAL AIR POWER

At 4:15 p.m., the President reached the PC. The sun had set behind the Palisades, and rays from the celestial star tinted the clouds above the 1264 with a purple and rose hue. The crew turned to honor the President. All hands saluted. The 21-gun salute was given without incident. And then the honor... The last ship in the line, the 1264, was the first on the President's return leg down the river.

TRUMAN HONORS THE FLEET

The New York Journal-American reported the moment.

Above the bridge nestled many small ships, destroyers, destroyer escorts, and submarines. The ultimate tip was entrusted to the USS PC 1264, too small to be given a name. But she was not to be snubbed on this proud day. The Renshaw circled her, and the President waved gaily to the crew.

Too small to have a name... A ship in the Mickey Mouse Navy... A small boy... All this was true. But there was a greater truth. She was a ship of the line.

The next day, Sunday, the PC hosted an open house. Visitors could come aboard. There was, as some reported it, a carnival air, an atmosphere of happiness and thanksgiving that the war, at last, had been ended. There was also "pride that this ship, small as she was, had contributed significantly to something more than this most important result."

Almost all the visitors were Black—fathers, mothers, grandparents, uncles, aunts, children, and friends. No crewmember was exempt from the deep pride that he was a member of the 1264. As some said:

Each member of the crew had established the ship's reputation and had proved that human ability could no longer be judged by outward appearance. It was now up to society to recognize this now irrefutable fact.

"I wish I had been there, Garvey, on the ship as the President passed in review. I wish I had stood on the deck and saluted the Commander-in-Chief and heard the guns give the 21-gun salute. Wouldn't it be nice to stand again on her deck?"

"That's quite a wish."

"A girl can hope."

There it was again... The feeling that Evelyn's interest in my research was true enough, but that there was something more... Something she hadn't told me. Something that still needed resolution... I couldn't get rid of the feeling.

"Garvey, such an honor."

"A precursor to a dishonor."

"What?"

CHAPTER 25

THE BLUES

"Evelyn, after the war... The Navy was downsizing from 3,300,000 to 558,000 enlistees and officers. It was time for the men of the Mason and 1264 to be discharged. It was also time for the final insult..."

"What could be worse than what these men had already gone through?"

"The 'BD.'"

"What's that?"

"The Blue Discharge, sometimes called the 'Blue Ticket.'"

"Never heard of it."

"It was a form of administrative discharge. Rather than providing an 'honorable discharge...' it was created in 1916 by the Woodrow Wilson administration to replace two discharge classifications: (a) administrative discharge without honor and (b) the unclassified discharge, which didn't indicate honorable or dishonorable."

"Between December 1, 1941, and June 30, 1945, 48,603 BD's were issued to men in all the services. Of that number, 10,806 were given to Black enlistees—an outlandish number given the percentage of Blacks in the military. Blacks accounted for 22 percent of all BD's."

"Post-war research indicated that two groups in particular received BD's—Blacks and homosexuals."

"Did the BD's make that much of a difference, Garvey?"

"A veteran with a BD had a hard time getting a job. Since the BD didn't indicate an 'honorable discharge,' a prospective employer felt he might be hiring a problem. Otherwise, why would the Government not issue an honorable discharge? There must be something undesirable about the individual. Veterans also had difficulty getting their benefits under the GI Bill because of a BD. The Veterans Administration (VA), which was charged with implementing provisions of the GI Bill, denied benefits to BD's. The VA's rationale for this policy went along these lines:

The purpose of the administrative Blue Discharges, which are not dishonorable, but are based on habits or traits of the individual that make his continuation in service undesirable and therefore the need to return them to civilian life as quickly as possible."

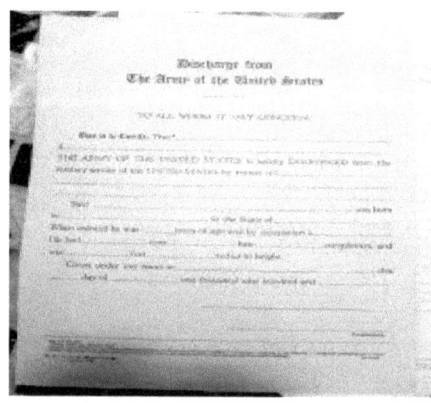

"There was no question that Blacks and homosexuals were lumped together by biased officers who issued the BD's. The Pittsburgh Courier, a Negro paper, launched a crusade against the use of BD's, rebuking the Army and Navy for allowing 'prejudiced officers to use it as a means of punishing Negro soldiers and sailors...' Along with others, the paper pointed out that a BD meant the 'veteran had not been convicted and yet had been separated from the military without being able to defend himself…' The paper stated, there 'ought not be a twilight zone between innocence and guilt.'

"The House of Representatives, pushed by the Negro papers, the American Legion, and the NAACP, took up the issue. The House Committee on Military Affairs reported that the 'effects of a blue discharge differ little from those of a dishonorable discharge… the discharged man finds it difficult to get or keep a job. Moreover, the suspicion of society is aroused against him, all the worse in some ways for carrying an atmosphere of mystery.'

"Blue discharges were discontinued as of July 1, 1947. However, the damage had been done. No one knows for sure if any member of the 1264 or the Mason received one. There is no recorded instance. But, as a group, Blacks in the military received far too many."

"Ugly. Mistreating people… Causing pain…"

"The times were different, Evelyn."

"I wonder how much different."

"Not a perfect world by a long shot."

"Of course, the world of 1945 was racist, discriminatory, and prejudiced, but not just against Blacks. Other people of color felt the sting of bigotry. As for a perfect world, that was asking a lot. This Garvey knew. This Evelyn was coming to understand."

"You might have received a BD, Garvey."

"Probably."

"So unfair."

"Evelyn, how about a trivia question?"

"Changing the subject? Okay. Why not."

"Why was the BD called that?"

"The Navy used blue paper?"

"Asking a question or stating a fact?"

"A fact, Garvey."

"Right. How did you know?"

"Blue water… Bluejackets… Why not blue printing paper?"

"So clever."

"If you say so."

"I do."

CHAPTER 26

INNER DEBATE

<u>TWO MONTHS LATER - GARVEY'S HOME IN SEATTLE</u>

"What did Professor Richmond say?"

"Generally, complimentary, dad."

"But?"

"Another chapter was needed."

"He insisted?"

"Strongly, mom."

"After all your work," Evelyn added.

"He's the boss. Life and death grip on my doctorate."

"What about the other committee members, Garvey?"

"Dad, they follow Richmond's lead."

I was at home. My folks lived near the UW campus. I may have told you that earlier. Great for my father... He loves to watch the Huskies play ball. The football stadium is within walking distance for him. Truth be told, I think he's a UCLA fan at heart, a closet Bruin in the "apple state." As for my mother, she just loved the area --- parks, quaint neighborhood shopping areas, and friendships built up over a lifetime.

I was home for --- and this is difficult to admit --- parental guidance. I needed to decide how to deal with Professor Richmond. That was my major reason for wandering back to my roots. The other was to again give my parents a chance to meet Evelyn. They had correctly noted the seriousness of our relationship and had hinted --- and not very subtly --- that they wanted to spend more time with her. If I gauged their parental motives astutely --- and I had --- they wanted a close-up talk with her, sort of an in-your-face type of talk… Mom wasn't going to give me away easily. Dad, however, was already won over. As for Evelyn's folks, I had already met them on several occasions and passed all tests to date. They, too, weren't going to release their pride and joy into my arms without a thorough once-over. I guess it's a parental thing.

In preparation for my return as the prodigal son, I took a long walk along the Puget Sound seashore, where I called upon my unofficial voice in the wilderness.

"Gramps!"

"Don't shout. Nothing wrong with my ears."

"Gramps, I'm between a hard place and a rock."

"Welcome to the human race, Garvey."

"This is serious."

"Didn't say it wasn't."

"Richmond wants some redo and another chapter."

"So?"

"I'm tired of it."

"Take a vitamin."

"He's too demanding."

"You just want a C-minus doctorate, right? Internet thesis? Classic comic book research?"

"That's harsh."

"Is it? Sounds like you just want out. Too bad the guys on the USS Mason couldn't ask for such a reprieve when those gale-force winds topped 90 mph, and 50-foot waves banged into the bow, almost submerging the ship."

"Gramps, you know that's not what I mean."

"Well, what do you mean?"

"I'm tired of it all."

"Sounds like a pity-party to me. I bet those guys on the USS PC 1264 were tired too, chasing a Nazi sub that could turn and sink them with a torpedo."

"Jesus, you're tough."

"What do you want me to tell you? Forget the doctorate. Tell Richmond to stuff it. Tell Evelyn you're not up to it? Tell your parents you couldn't handle the academic muck? Not this old guy."

"What should I do?"

"Garvey, you already know the answer. First admit it. The Professor, bless his bloody heart, is right. You need the last chapter. You can't leave these sailors hanging, swaying in the winds of history. You owe them! You know that."

"Owe them? For what?"

"For paving the way. For making it possible for you and Evelyn, and your mother to have opportunities... And for a host of others..."

"You're running a guilt trip on me."

"You think so? Check in the mirror. That harpoon sticking out of your conscience wasn't thrown by me."

Gramps was right, of course. Coming from a mixed family, as you know, I was both Black and white. To most people, however, my half-white inheritance still made me 100 percent Black. In an earlier time, that would have restricted my chances in life... But others had fought the good fight. I was beholden to them. I couldn't really deny that. Whatever I was... Whatever I would become was partially because of what they had done. No man, as the poets like to say, was an island.

Gramps was right about something else. I was feeling sorry for myself. I was tired of being pushed by my doctoral committee. They never seemed satisfied. Naturally, they justified their demands, arguing that, "they were trying to get the very best out of me." And they were right. They, I had to admit it, had pushed and shoved, motivating me to go where no Garvey had gone before. Truth was, I was indebted to them, but that didn't mean I'd say so in the town square.

"Gramps, I'll do it."

"Always knew it."

"Can't leave them hanging, as you say."

"Redeem them, Garvey."

"What?"

"There are souls to be saved, historically speaking."

"I'm not sure…"

"You'll figure it out. Now as to that other topic…"

"Evelyn?"

"None other."

"There's something…"

"There always is with women."

"Something, I think, about the 1264."

"Intense, is she?"

"Big time."

"Any thoughts?"

"Gramps, I think the past is haunting her."

"A relative on the 1264?"

"Checked the crew list a dozen times. Doesn't seem so."

"A family friend?"

"I don't think so."

"Women like to leave us guessing."

"She wants to ask me a question once the doctorate is finished. That's when, I believe, I'll find out what's going on."

"Be cool, Garvey. You don't want to lose this gal. She's terrific. If I were a little younger, I'd wrestle you for her."

"Two out of three…?"

"And the best man wins her. And now I have a question for you?"

"Shoot."

"Don't you have a question for her?"

"How did you know that?"

"I'm Gramps. I know everything."

"After the doctorate."

"God, I can hardly wait. You two should be jailed for teasing your old Gramps."

I think everyone should have a Gramps, or a Granny. Beats going to a shrink… Less expensive and you don't have to have an appointment.

"Dad… Mom… I'll turn in the last chapter in two weeks. It will be a home run. Start planning the doctoral party now. Have it catered by Chipotle."

"What's this obsession with that fast food?"

"Tastes good."

"Doesn't Evelyn work there too?"

"I also like her."

"That's obvious, Garvey."

"You noticed, sad."

"In a word, yes."

"I think we're embarrassing, Evelyn."

"Not in the least, Mrs. Langston. I'm glad Garvey feels that way about spicy, but healthy food. That's the way I feel about him."

I could literally feel my cheeks going crimson. That was Evelyn. Straight to the core... No mincing of words. One swing of the bat...

"Well, perhaps we should have a toast to Garvey's last chapter and the joys that will follow."

That's my dad. If, as some believe, one could budge the world with a large enough lever, my dad would do so with quiet words and a positive view of the possible. I still had much to learn from him.

"To our kids," my mom said. "All happiness..."

That was mom. A closet romantic... I still had plenty to learn from her.

The next two weeks were the most difficult of my life. I poured myself into the task. I barely saw Evelyn. She saw to that. And then the chapter, the last chapter, was done. I met her in our subterranean hideout beneath UW.

"Done."

"At last."

"Submitted."

"Finally."

"Want to read it?"

"Naturally."

CHAPTER 27

REDEMPTION

Redemption… That was the title of this last chapter. An old-fashioned word… You don't hear it often unless the minister is on a tear, and then the word tends to be slanted toward the metaphysical and the theological. That's not what I have in mind. I wasn't concerned about the hereafter. I was focused on more earthly, here-and-now concerns.

I was interested, however, in redressing the past—setting the record straight, so to speak. Letting the facts speak for themselves, yet guiding them toward the goal of righting historical omissions and prejudicial conclusions.

For me, redemption was not about revenge at someone else's expense, nor about showing them harshly how wrong they were. It is not about personal ego and the proclamation, "I told you so."

In the final analysis, redemption is about hope. It's about doing what we can to create a better world for ourselves and our children by coming to grips with past injustices. Not an easy thing to do, I understand that. Redemption comes without guarantees; rather, it comes with possibilities. It challenges us. Do we cling to our beliefs—our comfort zone of attitudes and behavior—or allow a fresh breeze to stir us? Redemption is, then, a moral compass, which, if we choose, assists us in navigating the past and steering ethically in the present.

Lorenzo DuFau understood this notion of redemption. Speaking years later about his experience on the Mason and the great experiment, he said:

"There were problems, but we just couldn't fight hate with hate. That wasn't our role there—to fight hate. We were there to prove ourselves. Nowadays, you see so many Black officers. To think that we were part of that beginning… It's wonderful to know that I played a small role in giving others an opportunity."

Going on, he equated redemption with patriotism—not the hyper-sense of chauvinism, nor the superficial concept of "my country, right or wrong." For DuFau, it was something deeper and more lasting.

"I have the dream of all Americans together. You're still American, under one flag, under God, with liberty and justice for all. And I believe that. I may be called stupid or something like that, but I still believe it. That was embedded in me."

Redemption for DuFau meant confronting the past, strongly and passionately, but without anger and hatred.

"From my school days on, I never had anyone preach hatred or tell me anything about trying to hate. I was always taught to love and respect others. Love and respect yourselves first, then respect others. It's so simple. It would solve so many problems."

A shipmate, Charles Divers, noted a sense of urgency if redemption was to be realized:

"The people should know what we did, what we were successful at. Even though they (the Navy) had programmed us to fail, we were very, very successful. Our success made progress possible in all branches of the armed forces. We were capable of doing everything that the rest of the general public was able to do."

Divers was concerned that the Mason's story would never come out. For him, that would have been a tragedy. All the work... the effort... the sacrifices... the desperate moments in towering seas... the barely checked fear of U-boats... the affronts... It all needed to come out.

"I feel proud that we were one of the teams in the forefront. We have to fight, fight, fight to bring that out. Us guys are getting up to... we're in our seventies now, and even our eighties. We've got to hurry up and get the story out! Otherwise, it will be buried. If we don't do this ourselves, it will never come out."

Arnold Gordon, another Mason sailor, related the historical record to redemption and the profound sense that a meaningful life should not be forgotten:

"History has proven that in the other military services, any real accomplishments by a Black unit were somewhat covered up and put on the back burner. So this was not publicized—our attack on a submarine—properly like it would have been done for other ships. They didn't want to give the Black enlisted men credit like they did the others. If they had given credit, perhaps we would have been looked at differently as a race after the war. I am totally bewildered that it's been almost fifty years since the ship was commissioned and the average public doesn't know that we ever existed. I still ask myself why."

Redemption came to the U.S. Navy in February 1945. As of that date, at least in policy, a new standard by which to judge Black people and other people of color was enunciated:

"The Navy accepts no theories of racial differences in inborn ability, but accepts that every man wearing the uniform be trained and used in accordance with his maximum individual capacity, determined on the basis of individual performances."

Redemption comes in many forms. In 1995, President Bill Clinton invited 67 living members of the USS Mason to visit him at the White House. It was there that each crewmember received a certificate of appreciation from the World War II Committee and the Congressional Black Caucus. Essentially, the certificate recognized and acknowledged the courage and devotion of the Mason's crew, both to the country and to their Black fellow citizens. It was there that President Clinton shook the hand of James Graham, leaving the former sailor speechless.

In 1998, then Secretary of the Navy, John H. Dalton, made the decision to name an Arleigh Burke-class destroyer the USS Mason (DDG 87) and to mark the occasion by remembering the contributions of the USS Mason (DE 529) to racial equality and desegregation within the U.S. Navy.

Only three members of the 529 could make the ceremony, held on April 10, 2003. The three were Winfrey Roberts, age 80; Benjamin Garrison, 80; and Horace Banks, 85. Prior to the ceremony, the three men were given a tour of the newest ship in the fleet. As recorded in the Port Canaveral Sentinel:

"The three men slowly made their way up a ramp, paused for salutes, and stepped down onto the 509-foot ship. The commanding officer, David Gale, said, 'Welcome aboard USS Mason, your ship.' Later in the day, they had lunch with the crew in the mess hall and were told that 31 percent of the crew was Black, a far cry from the 1940s."

A surprise awaited the three men after lunch. They were introduced to Mansel Blackford, an Ohio State University history professor, who had recently edited a book about the Mason. The name was more than familiar to the three men. They had served under Captain William C. Blackford. As fate would have it, Mansel was the son of the Captain.

They also met Pamela Davis, a technology operator on the new Mason, who was also Black and deeply indebted to the 529. She expressed her gratitude, stating, "I feel honored to be part of a ship that has so much history." Later, she described her feelings to the Sentinel reporter:

"It was heartbreaking to see these guys walk on board. It brought tears to my eyes. Without them, maybe I would have had to help integrate the Navy, and I don't know if I could have had the strength to do that, to go through what they did."

They also met Mical K. Crumby, Lt. J.G., who told them:

"I am a product of America's growing process. In the military, there continues to be encouragement and guidance for every member to reach his or her full potential, regardless of race, color, or creed."

Another sailor, Seaman Apprentice Imani Wilson, said:

"It's what a person does that makes history, and we, as a crew, and I, as an African-American Sailor, feel great about the job we're doing. If I have a hard or long day, I just think back to the crew of the previous Mason and it makes me want to achieve more."

Professor Blackford also provided all in attendance with a short history lesson. He began by pointing out that there were actually three ships named the Mason. The first was a destroyer, the Mason (DD 191), which was commissioned at Norfolk Navy Yard on February 28, 1920. It was named after John Young Mason, who was the Secretary of the Navy for Presidents John Tyler and James K. Polk. It was decommissioned in 1922 in response to the Washington Naval Treaty, which reduced naval power among the following nations: Italy, France, Great Britain, Japan, and the United States.

THE FIRST MASON

The ship was mothballed. In 1939, she was re-commissioned and transferred to the British under the "Destroyers for Bases Agreement" between the UK and the USA. She was renamed the HMS Broadwater (H-81) and participated in the Battle of the Atlantic against the German U-boat menace. In October 1941, after attacking and possibly sinking a submarine in defense of Convoy SC-48, she was torpedoed by the U-101. The ship sank with great loss of life.

The second Mason (DE-529) was commissioned on March 20, 1944, as noted earlier. She was named after Ensign Newton Henry Mason, who was killed in aerial combat during the Battle of the Coral Sea in May 1942. He was a graduate of the Columbia School of Dental and Oral Surgery. The school mourned his death.

THE SECOND MASON

The third Mason (DDG 87) is the latest ship to bear the name, a guided missile destroyer. This newest ship honors the contributions of Black sailors during WWII.

THE THIRD MASON

Before the day was over, the three surviving men were presented with copies of the ship's crest, along with an explanation of its symbolism.

The laurels symbolized "the honor and high achievement of the Black crew of DE 529 and marked their selfless contribution to the eventual desegregation of the Navy."

The shamrock represented "the ship's good fortune during arduous operations in the North Atlantic and the warm Irish welcome afforded to them during their port visit to Northern Ireland."

"The shield featured the Navy's traditional colors—dark blue and gold. Red, white, and blue represent our nation's colors. The two chevrons commemorate DD 191 and DE 529. The two opposing lions were adopted from the Mason family coat of arms and represent two battles. The lion on the left symbolized the Battle of the Coral Sea and the death of Ensign Newton Henry Mason. The lion on the right symbolized the struggle in the North Atlantic against the U-boat threat, especially the bravery of Convoy 119. The trident represented sea power and symbolized the DDG 87's advanced warfare capabilities, such as the Aegis Weapon System."

THE SHIP'S CREST

The crest symbolized many things. The helm represented a strong defense and the projection of sea power by the Navy. The anchor paid tribute to John Young Mason, who served as Secretary of the Navy. The cross alluded to the Distinguished Flying Cross awarded to Newton Henry Mason. The wreath acknowledged the awards, honors, and achievements of the previous Mason crews.

The ship's motto, "Proudly We Serve," was given by Black sailors aboard the DE 529 half a century earlier.

DuFau's personal motto was somewhat longer and perhaps a bit more provincial, but it was direct and on point:

"It's strange how you can fall in love with a big lump of steel. Only those who experience it can understand it. We refused to allow anyone to say disparaging things about our ship. You can say whatever you want, but don't put down our ship."

DU FAU ABOARD THE LAST MASON

———————————

"Garvey, this is wonderful."

"As long as it's adequate for Professor Richmond."

"Modest, are we?"

"Just glad most of it is done."

"Most?"

"A few last pages…"

What could I say? Every time I thought the last sentence was written, some new thought popped up, crying, "Well, what about me? Am I chopped liver?" And then it was back to the keyboard, thoughts jumping out of my fingers at such a pace that the computer software was working overtime. At such moments, I always wondered, "Who is in charge here, me or the past refusing to just fade away?"

I handed Evelyn the additional pages.

"This is it?"

"I think so."

"Garvey, should I take that as a definite 'yes?'"

"Yes, I think so. Anyway, you can soon ask me that question on your mind."

That stopped her. She grasped the pages, shot me a stern look before saying, "Go for a walk while I read."

DuFau's day aboard the ship included participating in a naval ritual dating back to the construction of the USS Constitution in the 1790s. It was called "stepping the mast." It consisted of placing coins or other items of significance under the step or bottom of a ship's mast during construction. Based on Greek mythology, the items so placed would ensure that the crew would return home if the ship wrecked during its passage. The valuable items would ensure payment of the crew's wages for their return to their homeport.

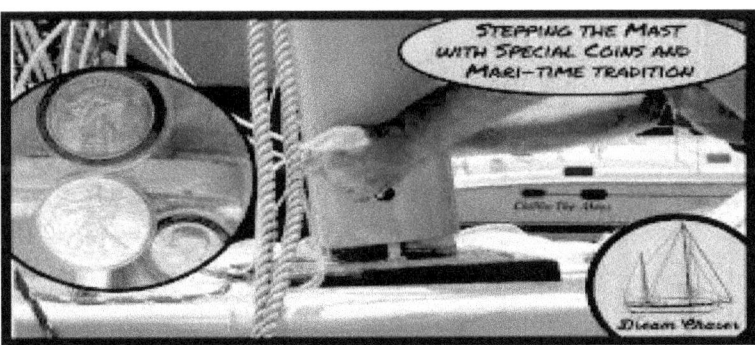

DuFau contributed his dog tag from his time on the DE 529. He said, "I wanted a part of me to be a part of this ship because this is a dream come true."

DuFau paused for many photographs that day, including one with Commander Adam G. Cruz, the commanding officer of the USS Mason (DDG 87). Also in the photo were Mary Pat Kelly, a retired Signalman, and Chief Raymond D. Kemp. More than words could say, the photo captured the new Navy while paying tribute to the past.

The old sailor added:

"You don't know how beautiful it is to see young people, all together, developing a friendship, and more than just a friendship—shipmates! You grow up together, and you're going to become so proud of your ship that you're not going to allow anybody to say anything negative about your ship and your crew members."

Continuing, he remarked:

"I'm so proud to be here today. Words cannot really express my deepest feelings because I become emotional when I realize the role that I was picked to play in developing America. This is America, a combination of all people, one nation under God."

He finished, saying:

"It's a very emotional day. And when I'm speaking and I look at these faces—the eyes of these young people and their interest—and I know that they are deployed and going into harm's way during a very, very tough time in our nation... I'm just so full of pride in America and who they are."

DuFau's day was not yet done. The vagaries of history were still dancing aboard the new ship. By chance, the old man was asked if he had ever heard of the "Golden Thirteen." His memory still intact, DuFau said, "No, never."

He was about to.

CHAPTER 28

THE GOLDEN THIRTEEN

While the Navy was conducting its experiment with the DE 529 and the PC 1264, it was also conducting another one. In January 1944, the Navy began an accelerated two-month officer-training course at Camp Robert Smalls for sixteen handpicked Black enlistees. The training took place in segregated facilities and under the tutelage of white officers.

The sixteen shared many common characteristics:

Most had been to college.
Some had advanced degrees.
Many had been high school and college athletes.
All had exemplary service records.
As a group, they completed training and testing with an average grade of 3.89, a figure never exceeded by any group since. Thirteen of the sixteen enlistees were commissioned as officers. They would be known as the "Golden Thirteen."

THE GOLDEN THIRTEEN

Why had the Navy decided to encourage Black officers? The simple reason was that by mid-1943, there were thousands of Black enlistees in the Navy and too few Black officers to lead them. Something had to be done.

Upon graduation, the Navy's institutional biases asserted themselves. The newly minted "Golden Thirteen" were given limited assignments, which included: (a) training Black recruits, (b) overseeing Black logistical units, and (c) commanding small vessels such as harbor tugs, oilers, or patrol craft crewed mostly by Black sailors. Sadly, they were denied the privileges and respect routinely accorded white naval officers. Not unexpectedly, when the war ended, only one officer stayed in the Navy. He made it a career, and before he retired, he established many "firsts" in the US Navy, including being the first to:

Serve aboard a fighting ship as an officer.
Command a Navy ship.
Be a fleet commander.

Become a flag officer.

Be an admiral.

Two things should be noted about this officer. First, he was not a member of the "Golden Thirteen." He was commissioned eight months after the thirteen others completed their training. Second, on May 23, 1945, he reported for duty aboard a patrol craft, the USS PC 1264. At the time, he was twenty-two years old.

Born in Virginia, he had attended Virginia Union University in Richmond. He enlisted in the Navy before earning his degree in engineering. He was among the first recruits at Camp Robert Smalls, where he trained to be a machinist before the Navy sent him to Hampton Institute to attend the Navy's engineering school. After completing his education, he was sent to San Diego, where he became a Fireman First Class (F1/c).

His name was Samuel L. Gravely, Jr.

For three weeks at the Naval Section Base, Samuel Gravely's training as an engineer was put to questionable use. His daily tasks included ensuring the barracks were washed down, well-swept, and sanitary. Later, he was promoted, if it could be called that, and placed in charge of the pool hall in the Welfare and Recreation Department, where his duties included maintaining the tables, collecting the five-cent charge for their use, and racking the cues and balls. All of this occurred while the urgent need for Black officers remained unmet.

In October 1943, Gravely was selected for the V-12 program at UCLA. This was a program for potential officers, allowing them to complete at least three years of college, a requirement for a commission. Gravely completed two semesters, from November 1943 to June 1944. He was then transferred to Asbury Park, New Jersey, for a two-month course to become a midshipman. After completing the course, he was sent to Columbia University to work for his commission as a Naval Reserve ensign. On November 14, 1944, Gravely was officially commissioned as an officer.

The Special Programs Unit decided to assign a Black officer to the USS PC 1264, an oft-requested position. Gravely's name was chosen, and he was sent to the Submarine Chaser Training Center in Florida for a three-month training program before transferring to the 1264.

Even as a young man, Gravely was acutely aware of the responsibility he carried as one of the first Black officers.

"I was sure that I could not afford to fail," Gravely later recalled. "I thought that would affect other members of my race if I failed anywhere along the line. I was always conscious of that, particularly in midshipman school and any other schools I went to… I tried to set a record of perfect conduct ashore and at sea."

Being a Black officer on the 1264 was not always easy. Though Gravely had a good rapport with the enlisted men, this relationship was eventually challenged. It was inevitable that he would have to place a man on report for a violation. After a Captain's Mast, the seaman in question received his punishment.

Retrospectively, the situation was nothing out of the ordinary. However, some of the men felt betrayed, thinking that Gravely, now part of the Navy "establishment," could not be trusted. Bitter words were exchanged in the crew's mess and living compartments. Gravely, however, remained calm and unemotional. In time, the crisis passed, but it marked another chapter in the Navy's ongoing process of desegregating and integrating its officer corps.

On another occasion, the ship's officers were going to dinner at the Officers' Club in Key West. The officers were informed that the town was southern and that many of the officers hailed from the South. They were warned that Gravely's attendance might cause problems. The PC officers, however, adhered to standard operating procedure: on the first night in any port, the officers would eat together at the Officers' Club, and that's what they intended to do.

Gravely, however, decided to excuse himself, claiming that he had a date in town and could not attend the Officers' Club. While it was assumed he did not actually have a date, the real reason was that he wanted to avoid creating any tension for his fellow officers.

Gravely would serve 38 years in his naval career, participating in World War II, Korea, and Vietnam. His career reached unprecedented heights in 1976, when President Gerald R. Ford appointed him vice admiral. Gravely was placed in charge of 100 warships and over 60,000 sailors and Marines based at Pearl Harbor.

Samuel L. Gravely, Jr. died on October 26, 2004. Six years later, the USS Gravely (DDG 107) was commissioned in Wilmington, North Carolina.

The legacy of Gravely, the USS Mason, and the PC 1264 can be summed up in the admiral's own words:

"Success in life is the result of several factors. My formula is simply education plus motivation plus perseverance. Education is paramount. Motivation: one must decide what he wants to do in life, how best to get there, and how to relentlessly proceed toward that goal. Perseverance: the ability to steadfastly pursue your goal despite all obstacles. It is the ability to overcome."

I timidly returned to the library. Evelyn was sitting at our usual table, the last pages of my manuscript scattered before her, clearly already read. Not really knowing what to say, I simply said, "Hi."

"I finished the chapter, Garvey."

"And?"

"It's good."

"Sufficient for Richmond?"

"More than sufficient."

"Good."

"And one more thing, Garvey."

"Oh?"

"I loved the way you ended the story about the bonding between the crews and the two ships. You described their love for the Mason and the PT 1247 perfectly. How the men came to care for nothing more than a big lump of steel and rivets. How they would never allow anyone to speak ill of their ships. If they were ever called a 'nigger ship,' they would proudly claim the title. They would be the best damn 'nigger ship' in the US Navy. No one would be able to put down these ships. Not now, not ever."

"I didn't go overboard?"

"You didn't even get wet."

"Thanks."

"Then it's over, Garvey? You're done?"

"Yes. I think so."

"Then I would like to ask my question."

CHAPTER 29

SISTER SHIP

OCTOBER 2036 – THE ARTHUR KILL

The sun climbed steadily into the morning sky, a reddish ball of solar energy casting its light over the Arthur Kill. The air was thick with humidity and the incessant buzzing of mosquitoes—hungry, persistent, and targeting the two figures floating silently in a rubber raft amidst the Rossville "graveyard" off Staten Island.

"God, they're everywhere," Evelyn said, swatting at the air.
"And relentless," Garvey muttered, fending off his own swarm.
"Was it like this the last time you were here?"
"Not this bad."
"I didn't sign up for this."
"Evelyn, this isn't some sanitized Disney swamp with fake buzzing sounds. Here, you sweat, curse, and try not to get bitten."
"You're so charming."
"By the way they're circling you, I think they like you."
"Thanks for the observation."
"Well, this is what you wanted, isn't it?"

Ouch, thought Garvey. That was a low blow. But it was true—Evelyn had asked for this.

"Garvey, I want to visit the graveyard," she'd said.

"Next year?"

"Sooner."

"Not a place I'm eager to revisit."

"It's important to me."

Important? Garvey had been floored by the word.

"Evelyn, I don't understand."

"I've made a commitment."

"To whom? For what?"

"When we get there."

"And until then?"

"You'll have to trust me."

Trust. The word rattled around in his mind like an unwelcome echo. What was he supposed to do? Revisit a place he'd sworn to avoid for a while longer? A place where one slip could mean a toxic bath, a run-in with a rent-a-guard, or a hefty fine for trespassing?

God, this was the last thing he wanted to do. Eventually? Sure. But now? And yet, she had asked. Could he say no?

What would it mean if he did?

"Gramps..."

"She's put you in a bind, hasn't she?"

"I'm confused."

"Love will do that."

"This trust thing... it's big, isn't it?"

"Pretty important, yeah."

"She won't tell me why."

"Would it change anything if she did?"

"I'm not sure."

"Will she go without you, Garvey?"

"I think she might."

"Well then, I guess you've got a decision to make."

He'd made it.

Now, the two of them rowed silently, maneuvering around the jagged, rusted remnants of forgotten ships. The Arthur Kill's metallic graveyard loomed around them—silent, foreboding, and as deadly as ever to a fragile rubber raft.

DANGERS EVERYWHERE

"Whatever you do, Evelyn, don't fall into the Kill," Garvey warned. "This area's water is a toxic soup—runoffs of asbestos, lead paint, zinc, and oil."

"That's an environmental nightmare."

"Exactly why there are no fish in the graveyard."

"And why those warning signs were posted."

"Right. No swimming, no drinking, no fishing."

"And you forgot the obvious—'private property, no admission.'"

"I never state the obvious."

"And the smell, Garvey. You didn't mention that."

"Tangy, isn't it?"

"More like dank and stale."

"Get used to it. It's part of the experience."

"I'll survive. Thanks for coming back. Now that we're here, I understand your reluctance to return."

"Each day, over six million gallons of raw sewage find their way into the Kill," Garvey said, his voice tinged with bitterness. "It's more than the waters can dilute, leaving them contaminated with industrial runoff and agricultural waste—basically an open sewer. The Dutch named it well. 'Kill' meant creek, but given the pollution, the name's taken on a much darker meaning."

"Give it back to the Dutch," Evelyn quipped, her voice lighter but no less sharp.

They rowed on in silence for a moment, weaving carefully past the rusting hulls of decommissioned ships, the skeletal remains of forgotten vessels, and crumbling wrecks of varying sizes.

"This place feels haunted, Garvey," Evelyn said softly.
"It is, in a way. Officially, it's a dumping ground for ships—dismantled, salvaged, or just abandoned. The graveyard of giants."
He reached into his bag and pulled out a photo. "Take a look. This is the Kill from a helicopter's perspective."

ARTHUR KILL SEEN FROM ABOVE

"Ugly. Looks like the scrap metal folks missed a few ships," Evelyn remarked, squinting at the rusting hulks around them.

"There's money in it," Garvey replied. "The Donjon Marine Company maintains the area."

"And doesn't want us here. A South Korean company, right?"

"Right. Which is why we snuck through the fence."

"Second time for you, Garvey."

"Never thought I'd actually come back. At least, not this soon."

"You hesitated when I asked."

"Now that you're here, you know why."

"Again, thanks for overcoming your reluctance."

"Couldn't turn down a beautiful lady."

"And the nightmare you had? The one you mentioned before."

"It catches me now and then."

"You never told me what actually happens."

The raft drifted too close to a jagged shard of metal. In his mind, Garvey replayed the nightmare.

The sound of tearing rubber. The raft collapsing beneath him. The foul, brown water, reeking of decay, rushing in. The reeds, dense and tangled, pulling at his feet as if alive. His sneakers sank into the muck, the mud sucking him down with every step. He imagined a creature lurking in this black lagoon, its shadow stalking him beneath the surface. Then, the fall—face-first into the toxic mire. The water invaded his ears, nose, eyes, and mouth. He flailed, choking, drowning while still above the surface. The panic, the helplessness, and then—

The screaming.

"That's about the time I wake up," Garvey admitted, his voice low. "Sweating, frightened, sometimes trembling."

"How terrible," Evelyn said softly, her face shadowed with concern.

Garvey needed to change the subject.

"Evelyn, it's time to talk."

They set their oars aside, the raft drifting in a pond-like clearing surrounded by the skeletal remains of forgotten ships.

"Why are we here, Evelyn?"
"To see the ship. It's important to me."
"I don't understand. You know all about the PC 1264. You've seen photographs, helped with research, even read the dissertation."
"Not that ship," Evelyn said, her tone sharp with emotion.
"What are you talking about?"
"The 1217, Garvey. The PC 1217."

Garvey felt a jolt of recognition. He'd seen the 1217 marked on an old aerial map of the graveyard but had never investigated. One PC wreck had been enough. Yet he remembered showing the photograph to Evelyn months ago and the fleeting, strange look that had crossed her face—surprise mixed with something deeper.

"I think I deserve an explanation, Evelyn."
"That, and more," she said, meeting his gaze.
"I'm waiting."

Evelyn took a deep breath, steadying herself.

"My great-grandfather was Henry Freeman," she began. "He enlisted in the Navy during WWII and served on the 1217 as a messman. Before he passed, he made me promise to learn about the ship—what happened to her after the war—and, if possible, to visit her. Maybe even write an article about her. I tried, but the records… they were destroyed in a fire before they could be digitized. What was left was fragmentary. I hit a dead end."

"What did you learn?" Garvey asked.

"The basics. She was commissioned April 27, 1944. She patrolled the Eastern Sea Frontier, escorting convoys from New York City to Guantanamo Bay and Newfoundland. Then came the storm."

"What storm?"

"The Great Atlantic Hurricane of 1944," Evelyn explained. "Mid-September. Winds over 140 mph, barometric pressure dropped to 27.75. It caught the Navy by surprise—five ships were sunk, and over 300 sailors killed. The 1217 was severely damaged but managed to survive."

"After the storm?"

"Emergency repairs in Jacksonville, then back to convoy duty. After the war, she was sold to the Maritime Commission in 1948. That's where I lost her trail. Until…"

"Until you saw the aerial photograph of the graveyard," Garvey finished.

THE 1217   THE 1264

"Yes. It was just sitting there among your notes."

"Serendipity."

"It was as if I was drawn to it."

"Tangible evidence that the 1217 once roamed the Atlantic?"

"I was excited beyond belief."

"But…"

"I couldn't say anything. Not then… Not until now."

"That was a good day for you."

"Garvey, I need to confess."

"You're really 75 years old?"

"No."

"You're a pagan? A Druid?"

"Thought about it, but no."

"You are a girl, aren't you?"

"My, you are observant."

"Okay, the confession, Evelyn."

Garvey steeled himself. Outwardly, he tried to remain calm. Inwardly, though, he was rattling. There was something gnawing at him, a sense of something he couldn't quite name, lurking at the back of his mind ever since he agreed to return to the Kill.

"Garvey, we didn't meet by accident. I heard about you from one of your seminar students. Good instructor... fair grader... That sort of thing. More importantly, I heard about your doctoral research. I figured you might help me with my hunt for the 1217. That's why I showed up that day. And kept coming back."

"Not my ravishing personality?"

"At first, no."

"But later?"

"Yes. Very much so."

"Initially, I just wanted to hang around. Maybe even help. I felt sure you could assist me. You were looking for the 1264—a sister ship. You were my best hope. Maybe my only hope. And then came the day I saw the photograph identifying both PCs. I wanted to scream, 'Eureka!' I wanted to jump up and down shouting, 'Great-grandfather, I found it! I know where the ship is located.'"

"But you didn't say anything."

"I was afraid to. I didn't know how you would react. I was scared you might think I was just using you. And by then..."

"By then?"

"You were important in my life."

Garvey's heart skipped a beat. He had suspected it all along, but hearing it said so plainly caught him off guard.

"Your interest in my research..."
"Always sincere. And then... Something happened. The story of the sailors on both ships—the DE and PC—got to me. Your efforts to bring their story to light, your desire to reaffirm their rightful place in history... Your willingness to wade through a mountain of documents... All of that got to me. I was hooked."
"On the research?"
"And on you, Garvey."

What could he say? Cupid's arrow had long ago found its mark, and now he knew the feelings were returned.

"We need to find your PC 1217."
"What about the 1264?"
"Over there."

THE 1264

Here's a refined version of your excerpt, enhancing the emotional depth and flow:

"I can see why you didn't want to board her."

"In the future, perhaps. Gramps can wait a bit."

"Who is Gramps?"

"Just a voice that bugs me now and then."

"Really?"

"I'll tell you about him later. Now, let's take care of your family."

"What's that ahead, Garvey?"

"A ghost."

The raft floated silently past the 1264, barely disturbing the still water. Garvey and Evelyn sat in quiet contemplation, each lost in their own thoughts. There was nothing left to do but drift toward the 1217, the ship that had brought them here, and yet, for Garvey, the past slowly crept back into his mind.

"Gramps, I want to board the 1264."

"Walk her deck?"

"The Bridge and the crew's quarters."

"Check out her guns... the depth charges..."

"Feel her under way beneath my feet."

"Once more on duty, Garvey?"

"The 'pride of the Navy.'"

"In time, Garvey. In time..."

"You know?"

"Well, you do toss and turn, and blather in your sleep."

It took a while before they reached the 1217, but when it finally came into view, the old patrol craft stood there, rusted, scarred, and weathered by time. Yet it was still floating, an enduring relic of the past. Evelyn's breath caught, and before she could stop herself, tears welled up in her eyes. She couldn't hold back the emotion. The long search, the years of uncertainty, had led her here, and now, standing before the ship, it was almost too much to bear.

Her voice, trembling, was barely a whisper as she spoke to the ship, as if calling out to the past.

"Great-grandfather, I'm here. I've kept my promise."

THE PC 1217

They drifted alongside the ship, moving cautiously, careful to avoid anything that might puncture the fragile raft.

"Nearer, Garvey. Carefully."

Garvey maneuvered the raft closer to the 1217 before saying, "Evelyn, you're sure you want to do this?"

"Do what?"

"I saw you pack the pennant."

"My great-grandfather's gift to me."

"And you want to return it?"

"If I can."

"It will be tricky."

"I have to try."

"That's why I stowed aboard a rope ladder and a weighted rope. It will be a climb. Sort of like pirates of old…"

"Garvey, before we do this…"

"Yes?"

"Your question."

"I was thinking. Wouldn't it be nice to salvage a PC? Find a good spot to moor her? It would take a lifetime to scrub off the rust, clean her up for inspection with a new coat of paint…"

"That's your question?"

"No. I would need a shipmate to help me. Would you be interested?"

In the best tradition of the US Navy, Evelyn answered almost immediately, and certainly with the brightest smile Garvey had ever seen in any man's navy, "Aye, aye, mate."

www.ingramcontent.com/pod-product-compliance
Lightning Source LLC
Chambersburg PA
CBHW051512120626
46551CB00012B/887